RADICAL

SMALL-GROUP STUDY

DAVID PLATT

LifeWay Press®
Nashville, Tennessee

Published by LifeWay Press®
© 2012 David Platt
Reprinted 2014

ISBN 978-1-4158-7219-2
Item 005471378

Dewey decimal classification: 261.1
Subject headings: CHURCH \ CHRISTIAN LIFE \
CHRISTIANITY AND CULTURE

Photo of David Platt: Allison Lewis

To order additional copies of this resource, write to LifeWay
Church Resources Customer Service; One LifeWay Plaza;
Nashville, TN 37234-0113; fax 615.251.5933; phone toll free
800.458.2772; order online at *www.lifeway.com*; email *orderentry@
lifeway.com*; or visit the LifeWay Christian Store serving you.

Printed in the United States of America

Adult Ministry Publishing
LifeWay Church Resources
One LifeWay Plaza
Nashville, TN 37234-0152

CONTENTS

THE AUTHOR

Dr. David Platt, the pastor of The Church at Brook Hills, is deeply devoted to Christ and His Word. David's first love in ministry is disciple making—the simple, biblical model of teaching God's Word, mentoring others, and sharing faith. He's traveled extensively to teach the Bible alongside church leaders throughout the United States and around the world.

David has authored several books, including *Radical*, *Radical Together*, and *Follow Me*. He's the founder of Radical (Radical.net), a resource ministry dedicated to serving the church in making disciples of all nations.

David and his wife, Heather, have four children: Caleb, Joshua, Mara Ruth, and Isaiah.

INTRODUCTION

High atop the Andes Mountains, the rays of the sun strike ice, and a single drop of water forms. It begins to trace a hesitant course downward, gradually joining other drops of water to become a steady stream. The stream gains speed and strength. Thousands of feet below and hundreds of miles later, what were once single drops have converged to become the mightiest river on earth: the Amazon. Flowing into the Atlantic Ocean at a rate of more than seven million cubic feet per second, the Amazon is more powerful than the next 10 largest rivers in the world combined.

In my first book, *Radical,* I explored how the biblical gospel affects individual Christian lives in the same way these single drops of water melt and flow down the mountain. The truth of Christ penetrates our hearts, melts our assumptions, and propels us on a journey of abandonment to God. In a world of urgent spiritual and physical need, gospel-believing, God-exalting believers don't have time to waste their lives on a faith that's been distorted by the American Dream. The American Dream prizes what people can accomplish when they believe in themselves, trust in their abilities, and work hard. But the gospel has different priorities. It beckons us to die to ourselves, believe in God, and trust in His power. The goal of the American Dream is to make much of ourselves. The goal of the gospel is to make much of God. In *Radical* I challenged believers to abandon everything for the sake of the gospel, take up their crosses, and follow Christ.

But you and I aren't intended to plunge down the mountain of radical obedience alone. The force of a single drop of water descending the Andes is minuscule. Similarly, as long as individual Christians journey alone, their effect will be minimal. But as men and women who are surrendered to the person of Christ join together in churches that are committed to the purpose of Christ, nothing can stop the spread of the gospel to the ends of the earth.

So in *Radical Together* I considered what can happen when we apply the revolutionary claims of Christ to our communities of faith. I contemplated the force of a people who come together to enjoy God's grace in the church while they extend God's glory in the world. I challenged believers to answer this question: How can we in the church best unleash the people of God in the Spirit of God with the Word of God for the glory of God in the world?

This small-group Bible study combines the truths of *Radical* and *Radical Together* to frame Jesus' call to genuine discipleship. Through these six weeks of study, you will learn what Jesus meant when He called people to follow Him. When you answer the call to radical abandonment, you recognize your desperate need for Christ and your utter dependency on His Word. You adopt Jesus' priorities of caring for the poor and sharing the gospel with the lost. And you learn to lock arms with other believers in single-minded, death-defying obedience to one objective: the declaration of Jesus' gospel for the demonstration of His glory to all nations.

RADICAL
ABANDONMENT

START

Welcome to your first small-group discussion of _Radical_. Begin the session with the activities below.

In recent years several buzzwords and jargon catchphrases have worked their way into mainstream Christianity. Sometimes these words and phrases are helpful for clarifying our beliefs or distinguishing a new way of thinking. Other times they aren't so helpful.

Place a check mark beside any of the following buzzwords and catchphrases you've heard in recent weeks. As time allows, discuss which of these words and phrases are helpful and which are harmful in today's culture.

- Seeker-sensitive
- The sinner's prayer
- Inviting Jesus into your heart
- Devotion (as in "I had a great devotion this morning.")
- Being in the center of God's will
- Quiet time
- Fellowship
- Something being part of God's plan
- Testimony

What are some other buzzwords or jargon phrases that you feel strongly about, either positively or negatively?

How does a person become a disciple of Jesus Christ? Try to answer this question without using any buzzwords or jargon phrases.

To prepare to view the DVD segment, read aloud Matthew 10:37-38:

> **"The person who loves father or mother more than Me is not worthy of Me; the person who loves son or daughter more than Me is not worthy of Me. And whoever doesn't take up his cross and follow Me is not worthy of Me."**

WATCH

Complete the viewer guide below as you watch DVD session 1.

We need to ask the question, Have we ever really come to Jesus on _____ _____?

Requirements for a Christian's Sacrifice
Jesus requires superior _____.

There is a dangerous temptation for us to try to _____ Jesus' words to justify the way we live.

All your affections belong to _____.

In comparison to Christ, we _____ the people we love.

This changes our _____.

It starts with a reservoir of love for the _____ of Christ and God.

Christianity does not consist of _____ obedience to Christ.

Biblical Christianity sees the supremacy of Christ and is so drawn toward Him that our _____ for Him drives everything we do.

Being a disciple of Jesus Christ means you forsake all relationships in favor of an intimate _____ with Him.

Requirements for a Christian's Sacrifice
Jesus requires exclusive _____.

Through the cross of Christ, we _____ to the life we live.

This changes our _____.

We are _____ constructing a building.
Count the _____ of following Jesus.

We are _____ fighting a battle.

Video sessions available for purchase at *lifeway.com/radical*

Following David's DVD teaching segment is the story of someone who is applying the principles of *Radical* through a sacrificial commitment to Jesus.

Discuss the DVD teaching segment with your group, using the questions below.

What struck you as new or interesting from the DVD segment? What questions do you have?

Take a moment to discuss David's central question from the video segment: "Have we ever really come to Jesus on His terms?"

Where have you seen an example of superior love? How did that love impact the people who experienced it and observed it?

What is the cost of following Jesus? How do we go about counting that cost?

Take a couple of minutes to think about a luxury in your life that may be preventing you from fully entering the battle as a warrior for God. What step could you take in the next week to remove that obstacle? Consider sharing that step with the group for increased accountability.

Do you think it's possible to live in the radical way David is suggesting? Why or why not?

Suggested Scripture memory for this week:

"He said to him, 'Love the Lord your God with all your heart, with all your soul, and with all your mind. This is the greatest and most important command. The second is like it: Love your neighbor as yourself. All the Law and the Prophets depend on these two commands' " (Matt. 22:37-40).

Read week 1 and complete the activities before the next group experience. Consider going deeper into this content by reading chapters 1 and 3 in David Platt's book *Radical* and chapter 1 in *Radical Together.*

RADICAL
ABANDONMENT

No one could ever accuse Jesus of being a great public-relations guy. Who else but Jesus would make it His practice to disperse crowds with difficult and controversial teachings when it would have been so easy to rally an army?

Who else but Jesus would choose to continually insult the power structure of His time rather than try to make influential friends in high places?

Who else but Jesus would align Himself with the lowest and the least of His society, those with no political clout or social standing?

But that's what Jesus did. That's what He's still doing. Perhaps with all of our educational advancements, the multiplicity of Bible studies and books available to us, and the abundance of churches in many parts of the world, we've forgotten that following Jesus isn't like choosing which flavor of syrup you want in your coffee.

The call to follow Jesus is a call to forsake everyone and everything other than Him. It's a call to a radical abandonment.

DAY 1
FOLLOW ME

Picture the scene with me. It's a clear day out on the lake. Two brothers are fishing, and the catch is good. They already know this is going to be a good day, and they're excited about totaling up the final catch at day's end.

They hear someone talking to them from the shore a short way off. They shield their eyes from the sun and cock their heads to listen. They're able to distinctly make out the two words that would change the rest of their lives:

"Follow Me."

Read Matthew 4:18-22. Why do you think Jesus called Peter and Andrew to follow Him rather than to believe in Him?

How are following Jesus and believing in Jesus linked together?

What did abandonment require for the early disciples identified in this passage?

"Follow Me." These two words contained radical implications for the lives of the disciples. In a time when the sons of fishers were also fishers, these men would have grown up around the sea. Fishing was the source of their livelihood and all they'd ever known. It represented everything familiar and natural to them.

That's what Jesus was calling them away from.

Look back at the passage again. What, specifically, did these men have to leave in order to follow Jesus? List those things in the left column. Then list in the right column what was represented by each thing they left.

LEFT BEHIND   WHAT IT REPRESENTED

By calling these men to leave their boats, Jesus was calling them to abandon their careers. When He called them to leave their nets, He was calling them to abandon their possessions. When He called them to leave their father in the boat by himself, He was calling them to abandon their family and friends. Ultimately, Jesus was calling them to abandon themselves.

The men were leaving certainty for uncertainty, safety for danger, and self-preservation for self-denunciation. Let's put ourselves in the positions of these eager followers of Jesus in the first century. What if you were the one stepping out of the boat? What if you were the potential disciple being told to drop your nets? What if it were your father asking where you were going?

Put yourself in the boat that day. How do you honestly think you would have responded?

What would have been the most difficult part of following Jesus in that moment? Why?

Do you think most Christians have had to leave much to follow Jesus? Why or why not?

This is where we need to pause to consider whether we're starting to redefine Christianity. We have to give up everything we have to follow Jesus. But slowly, subtly, we have reduced following Jesus to the *idea* of following Jesus.

We do this in all sorts of ways. We rationalize Jesus' demanding teachings: "Of course, Jesus wasn't *actually* telling you to abandon your family. And of course, He wasn't *really* saying to leave everything behind to follow Him." While it's true that Jesus didn't—and doesn't—require everyone to leave their father and their occupation to follow Him, He does require absolute obedience and commitment. Rather than joyfully embracing His call, we have the self-serving tendency to water it down to be theoretical sacrifice and hypothetical abandonment. We want to follow a Jesus that doesn't require anything of us.

Have you ever rationalized like this when reading Jesus' words? Do you remember a specific occasion?

Why do you think we do this?

In essence, we've redefined Christianity. We've given in to the dangerous temptation to take the Jesus of the Bible and twist Him into a version of Jesus we're more comfortable with. It's a Jesus who's OK with our materialism, fine with nominal devotion that doesn't require any sacrifice, and pleased with a brand of faith that requires attendance on Sunday but no real commitment in day-to-day life.

But I wonder if I could help you push through the haze of self-justification and ask a simple question as we study the words of Christ together:

WHAT IF HE WAS ACTUALLY SERIOUS?

DAY 2
A CALL TO DIE

What if Jesus was serious?

It's a haunting thought, isn't it? The implications are staggering. They shake the core of what we think we believe as Christians. The truth is that people in many parts of the world take Jesus' words seriously. People abandon their families and careers. They have to when they're threatened with persecution and mistreatment. They're living the truth of Luke 9.

Read Luke 9:57-62. Record what Jesus claimed was the cost of following Him.

How do we misunderstand these words of Jesus when we don't take them literally?

Three men approached Jesus, eager to follow Him. It would have been an evangelist's dream. All that was left for Jesus to do was to walk through the Roman Road or lead them in a sinner's prayer. Right?

But in surprising fashion Jesus seems to have tried to talk them out of following Him. To the first man Jesus said to expect homelessness on the journey ahead because followers of Christ aren't guaranteed that even their basic need for shelter will be met. To the second man Jesus said there's a higher priority than even the closest familial relations. To the third Jesus said being in a relationship with Him requires total, superior, and exclusive devotion.

Become homeless. Let someone else bury your dad. Don't even say good-bye to your family.

What do you imagine the response would be if such a sermon were given in a North American church today?

Read Luke 14:25-35. In one sentence what was Jesus' core message in this teaching?

Jesus never sugarcoated His message. He didn't play it down in order to gain popularity. He never glossed over it in order to increase His influence. He always told people the truth. But even after two thousand years we're still trying to find loopholes in the cost of following Christ.

That's the whole point of Luke 14:25-35: to consider what we're getting into before we do. Following Jesus isn't meant to be an add-on to real life, whereby we can do other things and follow Jesus too. The call to follow Christ is the only thing. It's all or nothing.

Read Luke 9:23. Why do you think Jesus chose the image of the cross to describe following Him?

This verse takes counting the cost to another level. In fact, for Jesus' original audience the teaching would have been even more scandalous. We lose some of the impact when we read it today, but for the original hearers the cross wasn't a bumper sticker or a piece of jewelry. It was a mark of shame and death. Crucifixion remains the most brutal form of execution ever devised.

Jesus was calling His followers to pick up an instrument of torture to follow Him. If someone was carrying a cross through town, nobody wondered where he or she was going. There was no hope left for them. No dreams. No aspirations. No hope of escape. Their fate was sealed.

That's what Jesus compared the Christian life to. It's first and foremost a call to die.

What parts of life are you still clinging to?

If you took seriously the call to die, what are some practical ways your life would have to change?

Carrying the cross has a finality to it. It's about giving up any claim on your life. That's what it really means to call Jesus Lord. It means He is your Master and your King. He has ultimate ownership over you, and that ownership transcends your desires, perceived needs, and dreams.

SO WHAT DO YOU THINK?

HAVE YOU **REALLY** COUNTED THE COST?

WHERE IS YOUR TREASURE?

We've been conditioned to expect not only having our cake but eating it too. Nowhere is this more visible than in our commitment to our possessions. Despite the warnings over and over in Scripture about the danger of wealth and money, as well as exhortations to give freely and sacrificially, we continue to find any way we can to justify our excess.

Materialism, maybe more than anything else, stands in opposition to the call to follow Jesus. It certainly did for the potential follower in Mark 10 who has come to be known as the rich young ruler.

Read Mark 10:17-31. Does this man seem as though He genuinely wanted to follow Jesus? Why or why not?

Does Jesus' response surprise you at any point? Why or why not?

If a man like the rich young ruler had come to you asking a similar question, how would you have responded? Why?

This guy was young, rich, intelligent, and influential. He was a prime prospect for the Kingdom, eager and ready to go. If we were in Jesus' place, we might have been salivating at the opportunity. Think about what a guy like this, with all his influence and prestige, could do. It's a no-brainer; we have to get him in.

Unfortunately, Jesus didn't have the personal-evangelism books we have today that tell us how to draw the net and close the sale. Rather than leading him through a simple prayer, Jesus gave him something else to do: "You lack one thing: Go, sell all you have and give to the poor, and you will have treasure in heaven. Then come, follow Me" (Mark 10:21).

Why do you think Jesus responded this way?

What does the young man's ultimate reaction reveal about the way he felt about his possessions?

Jesus is nothing if not consistent. It's the same call He issued throughout all of the Gospels to His would-be disciples: "Come, but when you come, leave everything else behind."

But let's not neglect the second half of Jesus' invitation: "Come, follow Me" (v. 21). Jesus wasn't just calling the man away from His treasure; He was calling Him toward greater treasure. This is very important because if we aren't careful, we can misinterpret these radical calls to abandonment and think Jesus doesn't want the best for us.

On the contrary, Jesus loves us so much that He's unwilling for us to settle for less than the best.

Reread the previous sentence. Where do you see that principle at work in the story of the rich young ruler?

At what point did Jesus love the man in verse 21?

Why is that significant?

Jesus looked at the man and loved Him. It was from this love that Jesus gave the call to radical abandonment. Jesus wasn't trying to strip this man of all his pleasure. Instead, He was offering him the satisfaction of eternal treasure. Jesus was saying, "It'll be better not just for the poor but for you as well when you abandon the stuff you're holding on to."

Read Matthew 13:44. How is the truth of this parable similar to the story of the rich young ruler?

Notice in this parable that the finder of the treasure didn't begrudgingly sell his property. Instead, He recognized the true value of what he had found and in joy sold everything he had. Why? Because he had found something worth losing everything for.

This is the picture of Jesus in the Gospels. He is someone worth losing everything for. If we walk away from the Jesus of the Bible, we might be richer on earth, but we sacrifice eternal life and riches. However, when we abandon the trinkets of this world and respond to Jesus' radical invitation, we discover the infinite treasure of knowing and experiencing Him.

THE QUESTION IS WHETHER

WE REALLY BELIEVE HIM TO BE **WORTH** IT.

THE TYRANNY OF THE GOOD

Throughout history individuals have embraced the value of following Jesus. Having done so, they didn't look with longing on the things of this world. Instead, they looked back at what they thought was valuable, only to be dismayed at their shocking lack of vision. There was no comparison between what they lost and what they gained. This is true not only for individuals but also for the body of Christ. What if the people of God, as a whole, began to see the immense value of Jesus? What if a massive force of Christians started following Jesus with reckless abandon? That's a world-changing proposition.

What are some obstacles that might stand in the way of an entire church's desire to live for Jesus with reckless abandon?

Describe a season during the life of your church when you felt it was close to this kind of abandonment.

What were the catalysts?

Did something happen to stop the momentum?

One of the worst enemies of Christians can be good things in the church. Of course, some will disagree with my claim; surely sin and Satan are our worst enemies. True enough, but we *know* sin and Satan are our enemies. We *know* we need to be on our guard against them. But too often we're oblivious to the threat posed by the good things we're doing. We've laid down our defenses against the way the *good* can hinder the *best*. In this sense good things can subtly become some of our worst enemies.

Reread the previous paragraph. What good things in the church might become the enemy of the best?

What is an individual Christian's responsibility in moving the church toward the best?

Read Acts 6:1-7. What principles about churches' priorities can you glean from this account?

Discussions about allocations of resources and church programming aren't a new phenomenon. Even in the earliest days of the church, believers had to meet together and decide what was going to be really important to them.

In Acts 6 the issue was the distribution of food to the widows in the community. The church responded not only to the importance of the need but also to the importance of prayer and Scripture. They looked objectively at everything they were involved in and reorganized to make sure the best wasn't suffering for the sake of the good.

But here's a key difference between that day and ours: we're not deciding the best method to distribute food to the needy so that we can have ample time to pray and study God's Word. Rather, we're deciding whether to allocate resources to bigger buildings. We're evaluating the effectiveness of the 17th program on the church calendar this week. That's the true danger: that we waste our lives on religious activity that's devoid of spiritual productivity, being active in the church but not advancing the kingdom of God.

Think about the time you've been a member of a local church. Have you been more committed to activity in the church or to advancing the kingdom of God?

How do you know?

Activity can't replace substance. As Christians today, you and I can easily deceive ourselves into thinking dedication to church programs automatically equals devotion to Kingdom purposes. We can easily fill our lives and our churches with *good* things requiring our resources and *good* activities demanding our attention. But these things may not ultimately be the *best* for the enjoyment of the gospel in our churches and the advance of the gospel in our communities.

To pursue the best, some of the good has to go. For that to happen and for the church to follow the example of Acts 6, we have to be willing, not only in our lives but also in our churches, to put everything on the table and evaluate it in light of a radical abandonment to God.

WE MUST BE WILLING TO SACRIFICE GOOD THINGS IN THE

CHURCH IN ORDER TO EXPERIENCE THE **GREAT** THINGS OF GOD.

PUTTING EVERYTHING ON THE TABLE

To experience the great things of God in the church, we have to put everything on the table. The budget, the programs, the classes, the vision—everything must be up for reconsideration before God. We must release all to Him and ask him to show us His priorities and purposes.

I'm not talking about biblical essentials and theological nonnegotiables. We don't need to change the words of God or the truths of the gospel. The church in Acts 6 certainly didn't.

Rather, this church sought to align itself with those very truths. The result was amazing: "The preaching about God flourished, the number of the disciples in Jerusalem multiplied greatly, and a large group of priests became obedient to the faith" (Acts 6:7).

What specific things in your church do you have the ability to put on the table for reevaluation?

How might you go about doing so without creating a spirit of disunity in the church?

The Word of God will tell us the right priorities for a church. In Matthew 16, the first time we know that Jesus used the word *church*, He made clear the mission of the people of God.

Read Matthew 16:13-20. How did Peter respond to Jesus' question?

Do you think Peter understood the implications of what He was saying? Why or why not?

How does Peter's confession of Jesus relate to the church?

This was a landmark moment in Jesus' ministry. Amid all the confusion over Jesus' identity, Peter boldly confessed Jesus to be the Messiah. Given Peter's words and actions in the coming chapters of the Gospels, he didn't fully understand what he was saying, for Jesus was an entirely different kind of Savior than anyone expected. He wasn't the sword-wielding warrior they were looking for; He was the Suffering Servant they never imagined.

Nevertheless, Peter's confession would be the bedrock for anyone—past, present, or future—who would be called a Christian. The church, and everything it is and does, is built on this truth. The church consists of those who have been called out by God to accomplish His mission.

This mission will be opposed by the forces of darkness, yet they will never overcome it. Despite that opposition, woven into the fabric of God's people is a commitment not to back down but to press forward in obedience to Christ. The church isn't meant simply to defend itself from attack; it's meant to push forward.

Read Matthew 16:13-20 again. How do you see the church defending itself today?

How do you see the church pushing forward?

If we want to push forward to shed light in the darkness, we must be unshackled from what holds us back. Put simply, we need to let go of some things. And we need to begin by asking ourselves some questions.

Are you and I personally willing to put everything in our lives on the table for Christ to determine what needs to stay and what needs to go?

Are your church and my church willing to put on the table every program we've created, every position we've established, every innovation we've adopted, every building we've constructed, every idea we've formulated, every team we've assembled, and every activity we've organized? Are we willing to ask God if there's a better way to use the time, energy, and money He has given us for His glory in the world?

Are you and I willing to say, "Lord, we don't want to settle for good things as Your people. We want only Your best"?

WHEN WE TAKE THIS STEP OF SURRENDER

AND OBEDIENCE TOGETHER, WE'LL FIND OURSELVES

BECOMING PART OF A MOVEMENT OF GOD'S PEOPLE

WHO ARE ACCOMPLISHING GOD'S PURPOSE.

RADICAL
GRACE

Welcome back to this small-group discussion of _Radical_.

What struck you as new or interesting from week 1 of the workbook? What questions do you have?

What specifically have you abandoned in order to follow Jesus? What specifically have you gained?

How would you define _materialism_ as a way of life? In what areas does materialism clash with Christianity in day-to-day living?

At the end of the previous group experience, you identified one step you could take to remove an obstacle preventing you from fully serving as a warrior for God. If you're comfortable doing so, share whether you were able to take that action and anything you experienced as a result.

To prepare to view the DVD segment, read aloud Matthew 6:19-21:

> **"Don't collect for yourselves treasures on earth, where moth and rust destroy and where thieves break in and steal. But collect for yourselves treasures in heaven, where neither moth nor rust destroys, and where thieves don't break in and steal. For where your treasure is, there your heart will be also."**

WATCH

Complete the viewer guide below as you watch DVD session 2.

A Radical Approach
Jesus' call to salvation demands total _____.

Salvation is never a matter of _____ reformation.

Salvation is a matter of _____ transformation.

If our lives do not reflect the character of Christ, there is a _____ issue at work.

Jesus is not merely a respectable _____.

Jesus is the sovereign _____.

A Radical Affection
Jesus calls us to give sacrificially because He _____ us.

Jesus loves rich people enough to tell them the _____.

God is a Shepherd who _____ us.

God is a Father who _____ in us.

God is a King who _____ for us.

A Radical Command
Jesus gives _____, not considerations.

Five Different Commands
1. _____. 2. _____. 3. _____. 4. _____. 5. _____ _____.

As followers of Christ, we do not consider _____. We _____.

Video sessions available for purchase at *lifeway.com/radical*

Following David's DVD teaching segment is the story of a couple whose hearts have been transformed by Jesus' love and grace.

Discuss the DVD teaching segment with your group, using the questions below.

What struck you as most challenging from the DVD segment? Why?

How have you been taught to practice evangelism in today's culture? What are the strengths and weaknesses of those methods?

In your own words what does it mean to have Christ in your heart? What are the symptoms of that condition?

What does it look like to live the American Dream? What are the symptoms of that condition?

Look again at Mark 10:21. Which of Jesus' five commands is most difficult for you to obey? Why?

What is a radical step you could take to obey one of Jesus' five commands this week? If you're willing, talk about that step with the group in order to get the wisdom and counsel of others.

Suggested Scripture memory for this week:

"If anyone has this world's goods and sees his brother in need but closes his eyes to his need—how can God's love reside in him?" (1 John 3:17).

Read week 2 and complete the activities before the next group experience. Consider going deeper into this content by reading chapters 1, 2, and 6 in David Platt's book *Radical* and chapter 2 in *Radical Together.*

RADICAL
GRACE

Perhaps this whole thing sounds too extreme to you.

"What happened to love and grace?" you might say. This idea of radical commitment and abandonment seems to contradict that. Right?

Wrong.

Our resentment of the demands of the gospel really reveals how little we actually know about God. The gospel, the greatest good news imaginable, reveals realities about God that we would sometimes rather not face. We find in the gospel not only a Father who might help us but also a Judge who might rightfully damn us.

It's only through truthfully delving into the gospel that we can find not only a real picture of the God we claim to serve but also an even greater experience and appreciation of everything He's done for us in Christ.

THE UNCOMFORTABLE GOD

I wonder if sometimes we intentionally or unknowingly mask the beauty of God in the gospel by minimizing His various attributes. Peruse the Christian marketplace, and you will find a plethora of books, songs, and paintings that depict God as a loving Father. And He's that. But He isn't *just* a loving Father.

Limiting our understanding of God to this picture ultimately distorts the image of God we project in our culture.

How many verses of Scripture do you know that relate to the love of God?

How many verses do you know about His other attributes?

Is it wrong to fixate on one particular attribute of God and ignore the rest of His character? Why or why not?

Read the following verses. Beside each verse, record the attribute of God's character that it presents.

Psalm 5:5

Isaiah 6:1

Habakkuk 1:13

John 3:36

Fourteen times in the first 50 psalms we see descriptions of God's hatred toward sinners, His wrath toward liars, and so on. All of this springs from the absolute holiness of God, His separateness from anything sinful. In John 3, where we find one of the most famous verses about God's love (see v. 16), we also find one of the most neglected verses about God's wrath (see v. 18).

It seems that much in the same way we try to soften the radical demands of Jesus, we also tailor our knowledge of the character of God to fit our own desires. Some of us might come by this innocently; maybe no one ever told us that God is wrathful and jealous for His own glory.

More likely, though, our inattention to the more uncomfortable characteristics of God's perfect character is an intentional blindness. We choose not to think about God in this way because doing so would require more of us than we're willing to give.

Do you agree with the previous statement? Why or why not?

How might reflecting on the fullness of God's character require more of us?

Do you have an unbalanced view of God's character? Place a check beside each attribute of God to indicate the frequency with which you think about it.

	NEVER	SOMETIMES	OFTEN
TRUTH			
HOLINESS			
LOVE			
ETERNAL			
POWER			
JEALOUS			
JUDGE			
GRACE			
RIGHTEOUS			
ANGRY AT SIN			
FATHERLY			
PERSONAL			
SPIRIT			
JUST			
SAVIOR			
SOVEREIGN			
MERCY			

When we either intentionally or unintentionally limit our knowledge of God to the parts of Him that we're comfortable with, we have the luxury of thinking much less seriously about our sin, priorities, resources, goals, and dreams. But if the Bible is true and God is who the Bible says He is, there's nothing we can rightly hold back from Him. He has laid claim to every part of our lives.

If we saw God as He is, then our lives would have to change. Dramatically.

But there's another effect of having a limited view of God, and this one is counterintuitive at first. When we don't see the holiness, wrath, and justice of God, we aren't able to truly experience the fullness of His grace.

Why might a limited view of God's wrath and justice lead to an underappreciation of His grace?

Ironically, we might choose to emphasize God's love over God's wrath, refusing to think much about the reality of hell and justice. We might even make the argument that we're doing so in order to emphasize just how great God's love is. But we're actually diminishing the very love we're attempting to hold up.

We can't fully appreciate the grace of God without fully appreciating the holiness of God. To put it another way, we can't know the greatness of our salvation without knowing just what we've been saved from. The Bible is very clear on this point:

WHAT WE'VE BEEN SAVED FROM,

BY GOD'S GRACE, IS **GOD** HIMSELF.

DAY 2
THE UNCOMFORTABLE ME

In order to realize the true goodness of the gospel, we must recognize the true character of God. When we do that, we begin to feel the weight of who we are apart from Christ. God's revelation in the gospel discloses not only who He is but also who we are.

Do you think of humanity in optimistic or pessimistic terms? Why?

Which way does the Bible think of humanity? Can you think of specific Scriptures that support your answer?

Read Genesis 8:21 and Luke 11:13. What truth about the nature of humanity do these verses present?

The hard truth is that we're all born with an evil, God-hating heart. One of the most poignant passages that bring this to light is Ephesians 2:1-3.

Read Ephesians 2:1-3. Record the words Paul used to describe humanity.

Is that too harsh? Why or why not?

According to Paul, we came out of the womb as sinners. That's our nature. That means our natural inclination is toward sin, not righteousness. Of course, no one looks at a baby and thinks, *What a cute little ball of sin.* But think about it: no one ever taught us how to lie or take things that don't belong to us. We all came to that knowledge on our own very naturally.

When we make sinful choices, we are simply living according to the nature within us. It's the most natural thing in the world. Day after day we exercise our natural impulses, spurning our Creator's authority over us. God beckons storm clouds, and they come. He tells the wind to blow and the rain to fall, and they immediately obey. Everything in creation responds in obedience to the Creator … until we get to you and me. We have the audacity to look God in the face and say no.

Now it would be one thing if we were the rebels in some dramatic, epic movie in which we were tossing off the shackles of an insensitive, abusive ruler. However, when you reflect not only on the power of God but also on the fullness of His perfection, you come to see just how heinous, destructive, and arrogant our rebellion really is.

In fact, you can't really appreciate the depth of sin until you've pondered the goodness of God.

Read the following verses and summarize what each says about the human condition.

2 Corinthians 4:4

Ephesians 4:18

These verses show us the true depth of our need. We are darkened in our understanding, and our hearts are like stone. We can't even see Christ because of the depth of our spiritual blindness. Without intervention we would happily stay on the path to hell, convinced of our own goodness and enlightenment.

God's justice and wrath are proportionate to the depth of our sin. And our sin is proportionate to the depth of God's perfection. Add it up, and you see that we are utterly hopeless cases without the intervention of God Himself.

When Jesus died, He didn't die so that we could have a better life. He died so that we could be rescued from the just and mighty wrath of God. Jesus took this punishment on Himself.

In your own words, how did God save us from God?

How does remembering this truth of the gospel affect our understanding of God's grace?

In the gospel God reveals the depth of our need for Him. He shows us there's nothing we can do to come to Him. We can't manufacture salvation. We can't program it. We can't produce it. We can't even initiate it. God has to open our eyes, set us free, overcome our evil, and appease His wrath.

In the gospel God comes to us.

IN LIGHT OF THAT, THE RADICAL DEMANDS

OF FOLLOWING JESUS START TO COME

INTO **FOCUS** A LITTLE MORE CLEARLY,

DON'T THEY?

THE GOSPEL RESPONSE

How do we respond to this gospel? Suddenly contemporary Christianity's sales pitches don't seem adequate anymore. Ask Jesus to come into your heart. Pray a simple prayer. Walk down the aisle and accept Jesus as your personal Savior. Our attempt to reduce this gospel to a shrink-wrapped presentation that persuades someone to say or pray the right things back to us no longer seems appropriate.

Think back to Matthew 4 and Jesus' invitation to follow Him. How did the first disciples respond?

Now read the end of Peter's sermon in Acts 2:37-40. How did Peter urge the crowd to respond?

Peter didn't ask the people on the day of Pentecost to "bow your heads, close your eyes, and repeat after me." You won't find a place in the Bible where a magical sinner's prayer is even mentioned. You also won't find an emphasis on accepting Jesus. We've taken the infinitely glorious Son of God, who endured the infinitely terrible wrath of God and now reigns as the infinite Lord of all, and reduced Him to a poor, puny Savior who's begging for us to accept Him.

You don't hear that in Peter's voice. You hear a thundering cry of conviction that says, "Repent! Recognize that Jesus has suffered, died, and risen again! Now flee from the world and run to Him!" The words explode with great power and urgency. This isn't an offer nearly as much as it's a command.

Look again at Peter's words. What does it mean to repent?

Why do you think Peter emphasized baptism as a proper response to the gospel?

To repent doesn't just mean to stop sinning; it means to turn. Turn away, but also turn toward. Turn toward Jesus! Turn away from the menial pleasures of the world. Turn away from the falsely satisfying lure of money and possessions. Turn away from anything that holds you back. But don't stop there.

Turn toward Jesus. Turn toward the fountain of living water. Turn toward the kind of obedience that brings true freedom. Turn toward a life that seeks significance instead of frivolity. It's the same call Jesus Himself issued time and time again.

Baptism is meant to symbolize the kind of death that all Christians are required to die. We rise from the water as a new person, a person who's at once dead in Christ and yet now fully alive for the first time. It's a public means of identifying ourselves with Christ.

In fact, in many countries even today the simple act of baptism comes not as part of a routine church service but at great personal risk. The person, through baptism, chooses once and for all to take on the name of Jesus. In a real sense baptism is an acceptance of the true cost of faith.

Describe the way you first responded to the gospel.

Having read about repentance and baptism, are you sure you're a Christian?

How would understanding the biblical meanings of repentance and baptism change the way you'd describe the gospel to someone else?

The gospel demands and enables us to turn from our sin, take up our cross, die to ourselves, and follow Jesus. Jesus isn't One to be accepted or invited in but One who's infinitely worthy of our immediate and total surrender.

Salvation is by grace. Absolutely. But that gift of grace involves the gift of a new heart. New desires. New longings. For the first time we want God. We see our need for Him, and we love Him. We realize we're saved not just to be forgiven of our sins or to be assured of our eternity in heaven, but we're saved to know God. We spend the rest of our lives seeking Him.

This is why men and women around the world risk their lives to know more about God. This is why we must avoid cheap caricatures of Christianity that fail to exalt the revelation of God in His Word.

THIS IS WHY YOU AND I CAN'T SETTLE

FOR ANYTHING LESS THAN A GOD-CENTERED,

CHRIST-EXALTING, SELF-DENYING GOSPEL.

SAVED FROM WORK TO WORK

It would be a grave mistake to use the truths presented in this study to support a belief that somehow you can be radical enough to earn God's favor. You can't. And the beauty of the gospel is that you don't have to. God loved you so much that despite your hopeless state of sin, He sent His Son—God in the flesh—to live the life you couldn't live. Jesus alone has been radical enough for God.

The starting point of your radical life is your radical death—death to yourself and death to every attempt to do enough for God.

Read Ephesians 2:8-9. According to this passage, why have you been saved by grace through faith?

Do you ever feel tempted to try and justify yourself before God? If so, in what ways?

Why does such an effort dishonor Jesus and offend God?

The gospel has saved you from your work to please God, and you are free from any effort to overcome your guilt before God. You can stop working and start believing. Based on nothing you've done and everything Jesus has done—by grace alone through faith alone—God has declared you right before Him.

In a sense that's it. There's nothing else. When Jesus said, "It is finished!" (John 19:30), He meant it. But there are profound implications of being saved by grace through faith. The gospel doesn't only save you *from* work. The gospel saves you *to* work.

Read Ephesians 2:8-10 and fill in the sentence below.

You are saved by _____ through _____ and for _____ _____.

The work of the Christian life is the often-neglected but nonetheless essential part of the gospel. Like Paul in the previous verses, James talked about belief "in our glorious Lord Jesus Christ" (Jas. 2:1), but shortly after that, he said faith without deeds is useless and dead (see v. 17). And in John's letter detailing the assurances we have in salvation through faith in Christ, the apostle said anyone who sees his brother in need but has no pity on him doesn't have the love of God in him (see 1 John 3:17). All three writers emphasized the necessity of putting faith into action.

To understand the interaction between faith and works, though, we must realize that the Bible uses the word *work* in two different ways.

Read Galatians 5:6; 1 Thessalonians 1:3; and 2 Thessalonians 1:11. What is the difference between the works described in these verses and in Ephesians 2:9?

In a few sentences describe the right perspective on work for God.

The good works in the first three passages refer to actions fueled by faith that bring great glory to God. Scripture is full of examples of faith producing work. Abraham's belief in God led him to offer his son as a sacrifice (see Gen. 22). Rahab's belief in God led her to risk her life for God's people (see Josh. 2; 6). Paul said he worked harder than others because he believed in the grace of God (see 1 Cor. 15:10).

Read another usage of the word *work* in Philippians 2:12-13. What is the relationship between your work and God's work in you, according to these verses?

When you believe in Christ for salvation, He gives you a new life of joyful obedience and overflowing love. So when you hear Christ's radical call to life, you don't think, *In the gospel I'm free to flout His commands.* Instead, you think, *In the gospel I'm free to follow His commands.* And the faith that God has graciously given to you begins to produce radical fruit in and through you.

You work out as God works in.

Are your good works motivated by a desire to earn God's favor or by the work of faith God has done in you? How do you know the difference?

True faith in Christ inevitably produces great works for Christ. But these works aren't fueled by the flesh in an attempt to earn our way to God. They're fueled by faith in a life that's abandoned to God. And all of it is by grace. The basis of our salvation—Christ—is a gracious gift from God. The means of salvation—faith—is also a gracious gift from God. And the fruit of salvation—works—is indeed a gracious gift from God.

THE ONE WHO GIVES THE GRACE ULTIMATELY GETS THE GLORY.

GOSPEL DEMONSTRATION

We have an uncanny ability to shortchange the true effect of the gospel. It's true that only by the gospel can we ever go to heaven. But the gospel does much more than change our destination; it changes the very core of who we are.

As we trust in Christ, He changes our hearts, minds, and lives. He transforms how we see, feel, and act. We begin to see the startling needs of the world through the eyes of a Savior who surrendered His life for the salvation of the nations. We live sacrificially, not because we feel a sense of guilt but because we have been loved greatly and we now find satisfaction in loving others the way we have been loved. We live radically, not because we have to but because we want to.

Imagine again what the impact would be if entire churches began to work for God, not fueled by guilt but by the gospel. The impact would be astounding.

Read Ephesians 5:1. How does this passage say the gospel affects the way we live?

Read the command in James 1:27. How is this command linked to the gospel?

When we adopt children, care for widows, or selflessly love our neighbors, we demonstrate the gospel. We tangibly reflect what God has already done for us in Christ. In a church that's radically pursuing God, the call to love and serve others will never be motivated by guilt but will instead come forth as people reflect day by day on everything God has done for them in Christ.

Why is it imperative for radical action to be linked to a firm understanding of the gospel?

What will happen if it's not?

Let's not act as if living the kind of life Jesus described in the Gospels is easy. It's not. It's hard. That doesn't mean it's not filled with joy, but it's hard work. It's a continual battle against sin and self. So where does the motivation for that kind of work come from?

The gospel is the key to—and the only sustainable motivation for—sacrificial living.

God hasn't given us the gift of one another to guilt us into trying to do a better job.Rather, it's so that day after day, time and time again we can remind one another of what God has done for us in Christ.

If you're a Sunday School teacher, a small-group leader, a parent, or a church member, the greatest thing you can do for your church is to remind people of the gospel.

List three practical ways you can remind people of the gospel in your church.

1.

2.

3.

We must also be careful that we don't accept becoming the kind of churches that constantly defend the gospel yet rarely demonstrate it. We must remind ourselves of the gospel but then embrace the implications of that gospel. As the body of Christ, we must be willing to display a devotion that matches our doctrine.

What is your church currently doing to point people to the gospel?

Whatever our roles are in our local body, you and I are fooling ourselves into believing we know the true gospel if our lives lack love for the lost or compassion for the poor. Together, though, we can beg God to produce the fruit of the gospel among us.

IN OUR CHURCHES WE CAN SHOW A GOSPEL

THAT SAVES US **FROM** WORK AND SAVES US **TO** WORK.

RADICAL
FOCUS

Welcome back to this small-group discussion of *Radical*.

During the previous group experience you identified a radical step you could take to obey one of Jesus' five commands in Mark 10:21: go, sell, give, come, and follow Me. If you're comfortable doing so, share whether you were able to take that step and anything you experienced as a result.

What struck you as new or interesting from week 2 of the workbook? What questions do you have?

David wrote, "What we've been saved from, by God's grace, is God Himself." What does that mean? How do you react to that idea?

In a world filled with needs, how should Christians decide which good works to undertake?

To prepare to view the DVD segment, read aloud Romans 10:9-15:

"If you confess with your mouth, 'Jesus is Lord,' and believe in your heart that God raised Him from the dead, you will be saved. One believes with the heart, resulting in righteousness, and one confesses with the mouth, resulting in salvation. Now the Scripture says, Everyone who believes on Him will not be put to shame, for there is no distinction between Jew and Greek, since the same Lord of all is rich to all who call on Him. For everyone who calls on the name of the Lord will be saved. But how can they call on Him they have not believed in? And how can they believe without hearing about Him? And how can they hear without a preacher? And how can they preach unless they are sent? As it is written: How beautiful are the feet of those who announce the gospel of good things!"

WATCH

Complete the viewer guide below as you watch DVD session 3.

The all-important question: Do we _____ this Book?

Do we believe what the Book says about the _____?

Will we choose _____ or a cross?

You don't come to Jesus as the means to an end. You come to Jesus to get _____.

Will we choose maintenance or _____?

Will we choose indecisive _____ or undivided _____?

Wisdom is found in obedience to Jesus, not in the _____.

Do we believe what the Book says about the _____?

Over _____ billion people are on a road that leads to an eternal hell.

Do we believe what the Book says about the _____?

Over _____ billion people live and die in desperate poverty, living on less than a dollar a day. Close to _____ billion others live on less than two dollars a day.

Close to _____ children will die today due to either starvation or preventable disease.

We are not inconvenienced by this extreme poverty because those stricken by it are not only poor; they are _____.

God measures the integrity of our faith by our _____ for the poor.

Jesus tells those with abundance that if they do not feed the hungry and clothe the naked, they go to _____.

If we live with so much _____, there's reason to question whether Jesus is really in us.

Video sessions available for purchase at *lifeway.com/radical*

Following David's DVD teaching segment is the story of a couple that is learning to respond to God's Word with radical obedience.

Discuss the DVD teaching segment with your group, using the questions below.

How would you respond to David's central question from the video segment: "Do we believe this Book?"

What have you been taught about the doctrine of hell? What questions do you have about that doctrine today?

David said, "God measures the integrity of our faith by our concern for the poor." How do you react to that statement?

What opportunities exist in your community for loving and serving other people in need? What opportunities exist for loving and serving others around the world?

Take a closer look at Matthew 19:23. What do you find hard about living as a disciple of Jesus?

If you've been convicted by anything you've seen or heard during this group discussion, consider taking a radical step. What can you do right now, before you leave this room, as a response to that conviction?

Suggested Scripture memory for this week:

"The one who gives to the poor
will not be in need,
but one who turns his eyes away
will receive many curses" (Prov. 28:27).

Read week 3 and complete the activities before the next group experience. Consider going deeper into this content by reading chapter 1 in David Platt's book *Radical* and chapter 3 in *Radical Together.*

RADICAL
FOCUS

The gospel is radical. It's astounding that a holy God would love notorious sinners so much as to be, as Paul said, both just and the justifier, sending His Son as an atoning sacrifice for our sins (see Rom. 3:26).

The gospel isn't just something that starts the Christian life but something that continually infiltrates every facet of our lives. The question we must ask ourselves is whether we really believe it.

If we say yes, then the only option for us is a radical focus on the Word of God. Not just an intellectual focus but one that's measured by our obedience. That's the true test of faith. We can say we believe the Bible all we want to, but the measure of our words will be our commitment.

The Bible must be the driving force in our lives and in our churches.

DAY 1
DO WE REALLY BELIEVE THIS BOOK?

Ask yourself this simple question today: *Do you really believe the Bible?* Of course you do, right? Maybe not.

For many of us, our belief in the Bible isn't much more than an intellectual assent. Although an intellectual understanding of the Bible is important, it can't really be called belief. Belief isn't measured by intellect; it's measured by obedience. If we were judged not by our words but by our commitment to do what the Bible says, our answer to the question in the previous paragraph might be different.

Based on your actions, do you really believe the Bible? Why or why not?

Consider the following areas of life. Write a couple of biblical truths about each one.

Money:

The lost:

Sin:

The church:

Now think about whether your actions line up with the truths you've written. Based on this evaluation, do you really believe the Bible?

We live in a culture that's always looking for the next thing. We're constantly on the hunt for the next stage in life, the next step in our career, or the next advance in technology. We're obsessed with the new.

God loves the new too. After all, He's making all things new in Christ (see Rev. 21:5). But if we're looking for new revelation from God, we're going down the wrong path. God has given us all we need in His Word.

In our lives and in the church, we're never without revelation from God. At all times you and I have His message in all its power, authority, and clarity. We don't have to work to come up with a word from God; we simply have to trust the Word He's already given us. But is that enough for us?

Is God's Word enough for most Christians today? Why or why not?

What about you? Are you looking for something other than what God has already given you in His Word? Why or why not?

What evidence would indicate that your life is radically focused on God's Word?

Read Matthew 4:1-11. Based on this passage, what are three words you would use to describe Jesus' opinion of the Word of God?

1.

2.

3.

Do you see what was happening? It was an epic battle between the Son of God and Satan. And what did Jesus see as sufficient? What did He rely on? What did He revert to? The Word of God.

This wasn't the only time either. Read through the Gospels, and you'll see the fullness of Jesus' commitment to and love for God's Word. The Sermon on the Mount is full of references to the Old Testament. When Jesus was making His triumphal entry into Jerusalem, Zechariah 9 was on His mind. When He cleared the temple of the moneychangers, He quoted Isaiah 56. Even in His last moments as He was being tortured to death on the cross, He quoted Psalm 22.

It seems pretty arrogant to think we might need something different. If it was good enough for Jesus Christ, I'm pretty sure the Bible is good enough for us too.

The Word of God is absolutely sufficient for us. Again, the question is about our commitment to it. Do we really believe this Book?

DO WE HAVE A RADICAL FOCUS ON GOD'S WORD?

IF WE DO, OUR **LIVES** WILL SHOW IT.

ROAD MAP FOR LIFE?

The Bible has been described many ways. It's been called a road map, a guidebook, and a love letter. If we're going to have a radical focus on the Word of God, we should probably be clear from the outset about the Bible's main intent.

What other ways have you heard the Bible described?

Is there anything wrong with these descriptions? Why or why not?

If the previous descriptions are accurate, then who is at the center of the biblical revelation?

The final question gets to the heart of the matter. If the true intent of the Bible is to serve as a road map for making decisions, a guidebook for your life, or a love letter from God, then the focus of the Bible is … you. It's a tool you can use to learn about your life, your goals, and your direction.

Although it's true that the Bible does all of these things, to think of it primarily this way is to misunderstand God's revelation.

Think about the word *revelation*. What, in your own words, does it mean?

What does it mean to say the Bible is God's revelation?

Revelation is different from discovery. To discover something puts the focus on you and what you did. It's about your search and your findings. But revelation is dependent. It assumes that someone knows something you don't, and you're completely dependent on that person to reveal it. Without their direct action you'd never know what they know.

The Bible is the revelation of God. It's a revelation because without it we wouldn't know God. And it's primarily about God, not us. God is the central character of Scripture.

Though the Bible tells us very practical things about life, it does so with the purpose that we can know and obey God more fully. When we think of the Bible primarily as a tool to help us in our lives, we neglect the true purpose of life as a whole. Furthermore, we place ourselves at the center of the universe. The Bible has a word for people like that: idolaters.

How would you describe your approach to the Bible?

How does seeing the Bible as a road map for life produce idolatry?

How does seeing the Bible as primarily about God, not about you, change the way you read it?

Our approach to Scripture reveals a lot about our priorities. If you want to know what you really treasure, take a hard look at the way you read the Bible. If you read the Bible with the intent of getting good advice, making choices, or finding your way in the world, then chances are you're worshiping at the altar of self. If you read the Bible as it was meant to be read—so that you can know, understand, and obey God—you're beginning to see the true focus of Scripture: God.

That's not to say the Bible doesn't have important things to say about us. It certainly does. In fact, the Bible is very truthful about us. But when we begin to read it with God in mind rather than ourselves, we begin to see the life and power behind the Word of God.

Read 2 Timothy 3:16-17 and Hebrews 4:12-13. Which phrase that is used to describe Scripture stands out to you?

What do you think it means to say the Bible is living and active?

The Bible reveals God's absolutely perfect character. As it does, the Holy Spirit begins to show you just how short you fall of His perfect standard. In this way the Bible cuts to the heart. It divides you, revealing the true motives and intent behind your actions.

But this focus on sin and self isn't for the sake of self-improvement or having a better life. We have to look at everything in light of God's revelation.

AS WE ALIGN OURSELVES WITH THE REVELATION OF SCRIPTURE,

WE DO SO IN ORDER TO PURSUE WITH GREAT ZEAL

THE SUPREME PRIORITY SCRIPTURE HOLDS UP

AS THE CENTER OF THE UNIVERSE: **GOD HIMSELF**.

THE WORD IS ENOUGH

Imagine with me a scene that is common in many parts of the world. You're preparing to attend a worship service in a country where the government outlaws Christianity. The Asian believer who's taking you gives you these instructions: "Put on dark pants and a jacket with a hood on it. We'll drive you into the village. Please keep your hood on and your face down."

When you arrive in the village under the cover of night, you're led along a circuitous route into a small room with 60 believers crammed into it. They're all ages, from the very young to 70-year-olds. The're sitting either on the floor or on small stools, lined shoulder to shoulder, huddled together with Bibles in their laps. The roof is low, and one lightbulb dangles from the ceiling as the sole source of illumination.

No sound system. No band. No entertainment. No cushioned chairs. No climate-controlled building. Just the people of God and the Word of God. But strangely, that's enough.

What would you think if you found yourself in such a situation?

How would you compare your view of the Bible to that of these believers?

What are some things in our lives that might dull our sense of need for God's Word?

It would be a strange scene to most North American churchgoers. What if we took away the cool music and comfortable chairs? What if the screens were gone and the stage were no longer decorated? What if the air conditioning were off and other comforts were removed? Would God's Word still be enough for His people to come together?

This isn't just a question for pastors and church leaders. It's a question of great importance for every person who claims the name of Christ. If we want to really follow Jesus, the only answer to that question can be yes.

Read Matthew 4:1-4. What does Jesus' response to Satan reveal about the sufficiency of God's Word?

Feel the weight of Jesus' words in these verses. He'd been fasting for 40 days. This wasn't the kind of fast where you skip a couple of meals but still have dinner; Jesus had been without food for 40 days and nights. He was physically weak from the hunger, but His words reveal Him to be spiritually strong.

So vital was God's Word to Jesus that He described it as bread. Food. The very basis of life. He needed and longed for the Word more than bread.

When was the last time you fasted from something? Describe your experience.

What spiritual benefits resulted from your time of fasting?

How can fasting be a means by which you come to a greater dependence on God's Word?

For many of us, one of the main reasons the Word of God doesn't seem as vital as it should is that our senses have been dulled by our comforts. We have everything we need or want at our fingertips. When we're thirsty, we go to a faucet. When we're bored, we go to the television. When we're lonely, we go to the phone or computer. There would be great value in intentionally depriving ourselves of one or more of these comforts specifically so that we can have a greater sense of what we really need.

Imagine what might be different in your perspective if you followed Jesus' example and fasted from something you think you need—food, entertainment, sex—and replaced it with time in God's Word. You fast from one thing in order to feast on another. Your body might grow weak, but your spirit will grow strong.

What is something you think you need that you could sacrifice for more time in God's Word?

In order to be radically focused on the Word of God, it might take drastic measures. We might need to actively remove some things from our lives to give the Word more prominence. It will be difficult at first, like someone who has existed on a diet of hamburgers and then suddenly starts to eat vegetables. But in the long run we'll begin to lose a taste for the meaningless.

WE'LL BE DRAWN TO SOMETHING **DEEPER** INSTEAD.

THE WORD DOES THE WORK

Second Timothy 3:16-17, in describing the Word of God, reminds us that the Bible is sufficient to make a person of God complete, equipped for every good work. The Bible is enough to equip us to live out the radical demands of the gospel.

Read Matthew 28:18-20. How do you see the Bible at work in the Great Commission?

Read 1 Timothy 3:1-13. Where do you see the Bible in the list of qualifications for church leadership?

In order to complete the Great Commission, our mission as the people of God, we must make disciples. And how are disciples made? They are taught to love and live out the Word of God.

For Paul, teaching the Bible was an essential quality for any church leader. Pastors or overseers are required to be able teachers. If you compare the qualifications for overseers and deacons in 1 Timothy 3, you see that the one key difference is the ability to teach.

In the church we're constantly tempted to think we need another program, a dazzling light display, or an engaging persona to make disciples. Strangely, though, none of these are mentioned in the Bible as qualifications for leadership in the church. Instead, Jesus told His followers that in order to make disciples, they must be able to teach people to obey God's Word.

Read John 15:1-8. How does this passage relate to the two passages in the previous activity?

According to Jesus, how is God glorified?

How does the Word of God relate to God's being glorified?

The sequence is obvious. We are to remain, or abide, in Christ. That abiding carries with it the requirement of time and effort. We are to intentionally engage with Christ, continually spending time in His Word, learning to treasure and love Him. As we do that, we'll produce fruit. In fact, we'll begin to be so conformed to the image of Jesus that we'll stop praying selfish, sinful prayers obsessed with our own comfort, and we'll begin to pray the kinds of prayers God delights in answering. And He *will* answer.

Through all this, God will be glorified. Understanding the importance of abiding in God's Word is incredibly empowering to anyone who wants to be radically focused on seeking God and His glory in the world.

Why do you think Jesus' teaching in John 15:1-8 would empower someone to bring glory to God?

Our ability to make disciples doesn't ultimately depend on our ingenuity, creativity, or experience. If we want to be radically focused on our mission to make disciples, we need the wisdom that can come only from Scripture.

Further, we need the Spirit who is at work in Scripture in order to draw people to Jesus. Our job isn't to change biblical truth, dumbing it down or making it more pleasing. Our job is to know and love the Bible and then to live out its teachings and commands, teaching others to do the same.

When you start believing that, the Christian life actually becomes a lot simpler than we make it.

ANY INDIVIDUAL AND, CONSEQUENTLY, ANY CHURCH
THAT WANTS TO BE UNLEASHED FOR THE PURPOSES
OF GOD IN THE WORLD MUST HAVE THEIR FOCUS
ON THE **WORD** OF GOD. WITHOUT EXCEPTION.

A CHURCH THAT'S FOCUSED ON THE WORD

The only wise basis for an act of radical obedience is the command of God Himself—the Author, Creator, and Ruler of our lives. Christians would be foolish to make radical sacrifices or take radical risks simply because someone in the church suggested it.

That's why dependence on God's Word is His design for all of us, not just for church leaders. As members of churches, we stake our lives—and His church—on truth from God, not on the thoughts or opinions of men and women. For this reason members of churches should desire and demand nothing less than continual feasts on God's Word in the church. This alone will satisfy, strengthen, and spread the church in the world.

Read Acts 6:1-7. How do you see this church being centered on the Word of God?

If the Bible is vital for the life of the church, why do you think so many churches aren't centered on it?

Would you say your church is centered on God's Word? How do you know?

As we read about the Jerusalem church, it becomes obvious just how important the Word of God was and still is. The church was engaged in the distribution of food to widows, and there was inequality in that distribution. The Jewish widows were being given priority over the Gentile ones, and the church leaders needed to make a change.

The true wisdom of their ruling was that they saw not only the importance of care for the needy but also the even greater importance of Scripture and prayer. In a day and time when the church is, by God's grace, reawakening to the great needs of the poor around us and in the world, we must remember that God's Word should be central in our ministry.

How was this church in Acts able to maintain the importance of caring for the widows without diminishing the role of God's Word?

How might their decision have actually resulted in more care for the needy among them?

The wonderful thing about what happens when a church prioritizes the Word is that it inevitably results in a redistribution of its resources. Notice what this church didn't do. It didn't say, "The Scriptures are obviously most important, so we're going to stop doing everything else so that we can really dig into the Bible." Rather, the church let the Word drive its ministry. Truly valuing the Scriptures results in practical acts of radical obedience.

This church's commitment to Scripture forced it to specifically devote resources to care for those in need. Their care for the Bible led to their care for the world. Their commitment to God's Word led them to a commitment to obey God's Word. When we unchain the power of God's Word in the church, it will unleash the potential of God's people in the world.

What are three ways you can help your church develop greater dependency on God's Word?

1.

2.

3.

If you're in a church whose love and commitment to the Bible are anemic, this is going to take time. We need our spiritual senses to be awakened by God's Spirit. Ironically, though, the way this happens is by choosing, in faith, to commit yourself wholly and completely to God's Word. You choose to believe that this Word is more precious than bread.

When you do, you'll find that this Word forms and fulfills, motivates and mobilizes, equips and empowers, leads and directs the people of God in the church for the plan of God in the world. Will we let it?

As leaders and influencers in the church, will we turn aside from our wit, our thoughts, our counsel, and our advice to give people God's Word instead? As church members, will we spend time in the Word, let it change our hearts, and let it drive us to compassionate ministry?

IF WE WILL, THE CHURCH WILL BE UNLEASHED AS THE MASSIVE FORCE FOR **GOD'S GLORY** THAT IT WAS MEANT TO BE.

RADICAL STRATEGY

Welcome back to this small-group discussion of *Radical*.

What struck you as new or interesting from week 3 of the workbook? What questions do you have?

During what season of life have you been most influenced by God's Word?

What obstacles have regularly limited the impact of God's Word in your life?

Is it reasonable to expect Christians to successfully understand, interpret, and apply the Bible? Why or why not?

To prepare to view the DVD segment, read aloud 2 Corinthians 1:3-7:

"Praise the God and Father of our Lord Jesus Christ, the Father of mercies and the God of all comfort. He comforts us in all our affliction, so that we may be able to comfort those who are in any kind of affliction, through the comfort we ourselves receive from God. For as the sufferings of Christ overflow to us, so through Christ our comfort also overflows. If we are afflicted, it is for your comfort and salvation. If we are comforted, it is for your comfort, which is experienced in your endurance of the same sufferings that we suffer. And our hope for you is firm, because we know that as you share in the sufferings, so you will share in the comfort."

WATCH

Complete the viewer guide below as you watch DVD session 4.

Two Ingredients of Radical Compassion

1. Supernatural _____ of the condition of the lost

2. Sacrificial _____ to the commission of Christ

The Condition of the Lost

See their _____.

Over _____ billion people are on a road that leads to an eternal hell.

The Condition of the Lost

Feel their _____.

The only way you and I can ever have this kind of compassion is if _____ is in us.

The Condition of the Lost

Realize their _____.

We need God to deliver us from natural affections to a supernatural awareness of the condition of the _____.

The Commission of Christ

Jesus beckons us to _____.

Jesus summons us to _____.

Video sessions available for purchase at *lifeway.com/radical*

RESPOND

Following David's DVD teaching segment is the story of someone who is applying the principles of *Radical* by taking the good news of Jesus to lost people.

Discuss the DVD teaching segment with your group, using the questions below.

What did you find most intriguing about the DVD segment? Why?

In recent years when have you felt deep compassion for another person or for a group of people? What do you remember most about that experience?

Which sins (committed by yourself or by others) make you feel repulsed? Which sins make you feel compassionate?

Why is prayer a vital part of serving and witnessing to the lost?

What would it take for you to know for sure that you'd been called to go and serve God in another country? What would it take for you to obey that call?

Take a minute to identify one person within your sphere of influence who needs to encounter Jesus Christ. Commit to pray for that person's eternal salvation every day this week. Consider verbally expressing your commitment to the group for increased accountability.

Suggested Scripture memory for this week:

"Everyone who will acknowledge Me before men, I will also acknowledge him before My Father in heaven. But whoever denies Me before men, I will also deny him before My Father in heaven" (Matt. 10:32-33).

Read week 4 and complete the activities before the next group experience. Consider going deeper into this content by reading chapter 5 in David Platt's book *Radical* and chapter 4 in *Radical Together.*

RADICAL
STRATEGY

A radical focus on Scripture will result in the church's moving out to fulfill its God-given mission on earth. So what is that mission?

In Jesus' simple command to make disciples (see Matt. 28:18-20), He invited each of His followers to share the life of Christ with others through a sacrificial, intentional, global effort to spread the gospel.

The church isn't meant to gather people together as much as it's meant to send people out into the world. That means you. And me. And everyone else who is called a Christian. The goal of the church is never for one person to be equipped and empowered to lead as many people as possible to Christ. The goal is always for all of God's people to be equipped and empowered to lead as many people as possible to Christ.

Not just in here. But out there.

DAY 1
A DISCIPLE-MAKING LIFE

Jesus stood on the mountain, ready to ascend into heaven, and gave His marching orders to the disciples: "All authority has been given to Me in heaven and on earth. Go, therefore, and make disciples of all nations, baptizing them in the name of the Father and of the Son and of the Holy Spirit, teaching them to observe everything I have commanded you. And remember, I am with you always, to the end of the age" (Matt. 28:18-20).

Jesus never intended to limit this invitation to the most effective communicators, the most brilliant organizers, or the most talented leaders and artists—all of the allegedly right people whom you and I are prone to exalt in the church. Rather, this statement is meant for everyone. We are all called to make disciples.

Have you ever thought of yourself as a disciple maker? Why or why not?

Why do you think we tend to assign this task primarily to those who serve in a vocational role in the church?

If the 11 disciples standing there were to teach all nations to observe everything Jesus had commanded them, then that had to include what Jesus was commanding them that day. Part of making disciples for that initial group was to tell others to make disciples. Then those disciples were to tell new disciples to make disciples, and on and on.

Unfortunately, you can look around Christianity today and find a definite divide between lay people and professional Christians. Where did we get the idea that some people are specifically charged with the disciple-making task while others are not? Certainly not from Jesus.

What excuses might people give for not being involved in making disciples?

Are any of these valid? Why or why not?

It's surprising when you think about the people to whom Jesus entrusted this mission. Fishers? Reformed tax collectors? A prostitute? It's hardly the core group most church planters dream of today. Jesus didn't seem too worried, though. Perhaps that's because these "wrong" people were more ready for the mission than they realized.

During His ministry on earth, Jesus spent more time with 12 men than with everyone else put together. In John 17, when Jesus recounted His ministry before going to the cross, He didn't mention the multitudes He'd preached to or the miracles He'd performed. As spectacular as those events were, they weren't His primary focus. Instead, 40 times Jesus spoke to and about the men in whom He'd invested His life. They were His focus.

Scan Jesus' High Priestly prayer in John 17. List some ways He prayed for His disciples.

If you followed Jesus' example of making disciples, how would you need to start spending your time?

What kinds of practical things in your life might need to be rearranged for you to intentionally make disciples?

You're called to make disciples. So am I. But we must be intentional about doing so. Disciples aren't made by accident, but the process might be simpler than you realize. Think back to Jesus' example.

Jesus commanded His followers to do with others what He had done with them. Jesus didn't sit in a classroom; He shared His life. He walked and talked and ate with them, and at every turn He taught them about the kingdom of God. You can do the same.

Instead of seeing your ordinary activities as simply things to be done, follow Jesus' example and start seeing them as opportunities to make disciples. Don't just go to the grocery store by yourself; take someone with you and talk about stewardship of resources. Then don't just buy food for yourself; buy a little less so that you can buy some for someone else.

When someone comes over to babysit your children, don't just give them a check and send them home. Engage them in conversation. Talk about their lives and their spiritual development. Begin to embrace the ordinary opportunities for the extraordinary act of making disciples.

What is one way you can begin to make disciples?

Like you, I'm constantly beset by the busyness of life. If I'm not careful, disciple making fades into the background.

INTENTIONALITY IS VITAL TO A RADICAL

DISCIPLE-MAKING STRATEGY.

DAY 2
A CHURCH OUT THERE

The beauty of God's plan to reach the nations with the gospel is that it doesn't depend on programs, buildings, or professionals. If spreading the gospel depends on these things, we'll never reach the ends of the earth. We'll never have enough resources, staff, buildings, events, or activities to reach all of the people in our communities, much less all of the people in the world.

Unfortunately, most of us feel these things are necessary to accomplish God's mission.

Read 1 Corinthians 3:16; 6:18-20. How did Paul describe Christians in these verses?

Why is that identity important to remember as you think about completing God's mission?

Before Christ came, the Jewish people were used to seeing God's presence symbolized in the temple, a monumental edifice. But with Jesus' death on the cross, the way was opened for people to dwell in God's presence in any place. No central building was necessary. As a result, they no longer needed to focus on a building as a house of worship.

Then what would the house of worship be?

You guessed it: people. The astounding reality of New Testament Christianity is that we, as believers, are the house of worship. It seems clear that God has chosen to devote His energy to building these houses of worship. Why, then, are we so bent on spending the bulk of energy to build something else?

Why do you think we are so preoccupied with building large churches?

How would the life of your church change if suddenly there were no building?

What does your answer reveal about your priorities in the church?

We would do well to consider that many of our Christian brothers and sisters around the world simply meet outside. Let's at least consider not spending such a large portion of our resources on building places when the priority of the New Testament is decidedly on building people.

Sure, there are advantages to having a nice church building. But when we have an unhealthy occupation with buildings and what happens there, we neglect the fact that Jesus called the church not to be in here but to be out there.

What attitudes stand in the way of the church's being out there in the world?

What tangible things stand in the way?

Read Acts 1:8; 8:1. Why was the church scattered in Acts 8:1?

The pull inward is very strong in a church. Inside the building almost everyone thinks the way we do. They talk the way we do. There aren't many arguments or disagreements. We are free from dangerous influences in the world. It's safe and comfortable inside.

The Jerusalem church felt the inward pull too. Though Jesus told them in Acts 1 to be His witnesses all around the known world, they were still hanging around Jerusalem at the beginning of Acts 8. It wasn't until Stephen's death and a wave of persecution broke out that they actually began to scatter.

Our natural inclination is to turn inward. We must consciously choose, then, to turn our focus outward. It's much more dangerous and confrontational out there, but out there is where Christ has called us to share His gospel.

THE REAL QUESTION WE NEED TO ASK OURSELVES, AS THE CHURCH, IS WHETHER WE ARE SPENDING OUR RESOURCES TO MAKE "IN HERE" MORE COMFORTABLE OR WHETHER WE ARE EXHORTING ONE ANOTHER TO CONTINUALLY BE **"OUT THERE."**

GREATER THINGS

A crowd gathered to watch the scene as the early disciples burst out of the upper room. They had never seen or heard anything like it. They were hearing the gospel in their own languages from ordinary, unschooled, ragtag nobodies.

When you read Acts 2, you realize the giving of the Spirit wasn't a special anointing on a select few but a supernatural anointing on every one of God's people.

Read Joel 2:28-29. How was this prophecy fulfilled in Acts 2?

Do you often think of yourself as being anointed with the Holy Spirit? Why or why not?

All men and women who have placed their faith in Christ have the Spirit living in them so that they can be witnesses for Christ to the ends of the earth. Jesus pointed to this truth when He talked with His disciples about the coming of the Holy Spirit.

Read John 14:12. In your own words, what was Jesus saying in this passage?

What do you think He meant by "greater works"?

Was Jesus saying the anointing of the Holy Spirit on us would be stronger than it was on Him? The Spirit's anointing on us isn't stronger in quality than it was on Jesus. After all, He was sinless, and as a result, His relationship with the Spirit of God was totally unhindered. So how will the Spirit's anointing on our lives enable us to do greater things than Jesus could do?

We will do greater things, not because of the quality of the Spirit in select believers among us but because the Spirit is spread throughout all of us in the body of Christ. This is a monumental change from the way God had operated in history.

Read the following passages. Beside each one record the work of the Spirit.

Exodus 31:2-4

Numbers 11:25

Judges 3:10

1 Kings 18:12

How is the picture of the Holy Spirit in these Old Testament Scriptures different from the one in Acts 2?

In the Old Testament the Spirit of God came for a specific time and occasion and to a particular individual. Beginning in Acts 2, the Spirit of God began to rest on every disciple of Jesus, and because of the filling of the Spirit all across the community of faith, we can see greater things than anyone ever saw in Jesus' ministry.

At this moment, as you read this sentence, men and women around the world are being saved from their sins through the proclamation of the gospel. People are being delivered from addictions and healed of diseases. Brothers and sisters are advancing the gospel in power amid unreached people groups. All this is happening because the Spirit of God has been poured out on all of His people all over the world.

How does your belief in the indwelling Holy Spirit change the way you view other members of your church?

How does it change the way you see yourself?

If the remaining 11 disciples, indwelled by the Holy Spirit, were enough to carry the gospel to the ends of the earth, a church with even a handful of members can spread the gospel in and beyond a community.

THOSE ARE THE GREATER THINGS JESUS SAID WE WOULD DO.

AND THOSE GREATER THINGS ARE FOR EVERY CHRISTIAN.

THE NECESSITY OF ALL

Because God has poured out the Holy Spirit onto all Christians, it's unthinkable to look around your faith community and assign lesser value to any individual in favor of anyone else. If we want to complete Jesus' mission, we're all essential.

Read Romans 12:3-8. What reasons did Paul give for not thinking of one part of the body of Christ more highly than the others?

Have you ever been tempted to assign greater importance to one part of the church over another? Why do you think that temptation is so strong?

Regardless of your place in the church, remember that God didn't intend for you to be sidelined in His kingdom. At times you may feel like the wrong person, thinking you're not gifted enough, smart enough, talented enough, or qualified enough to engage in effective ministry. This simply isn't true.

If you believe you're not good enough to minister, is your self-esteem the cause? If not, what is?

How would engaging in the kingdom be an expression of faith?

You may have been told lies throughout your life about your ordinariness, unimportance, or insignificance. But if you believe that, I urge you to take another look at the Bible and believe what it says about you.

Read 1 Corinthians 12:12-27. How does this passage refute any feelings of insignificance you might harbor?

You have the Word of God before you, the Spirit of God in you, and the command of God to you: make disciples of all nations. So whether you are a businessperson, a lawyer, a doctor, a consultant, a construction worker, a teacher, a student, an on-the-go professional, or a busy mom, I implore you to ask God to make your life count where you live for the advance of the gospel and the declaration of His glory to the ends of the earth.

That might sound like too big a vision. It's not. If you start looking around, there are more opportunities for you to impact the world than you might imagine. In order to inform your vision, though, it's worth asking yourself some questions of belief stemming from Psalm 139.

Read Psalm 139:1-16. What characteristics of God do these verses emphasize?

If you really believed these things, how would they affect the way you view your current life situation?

Do you really believe God has directed your path into your current apartment or neighborhood? Do you really believe your physical makeup is intentionally designed? And do you really believe you can go nowhere apart from the presence of God because He lives inside you through the Holy Spirit? If you believe these things, the place you're sitting right now is no accident.

Neither is where you buy your gas. Or your fast food. Or the relationships you're in. There's divine intentionality behind it. Consider where God has placed you, whom God has put around you, and how God wants to use you for His glory where you live and work.

Identify some specific aspects of your life and character that you think God designed for ministry and witness.

If you're single, how can you make the most of your singleness for ministry? If you're married, how can you serve together with your spouse in your community? If you have kids, how can you make your home a ministry to children in your neighborhood? If you work outside the home, how can you share Christ in your workplace? All of these avenues are open to you.

IF ALL OF US IN THE CHURCH EMBRACE WHAT GOD HAS PUT

IN US AND BEFORE US, A TIDAL WAVE OF GOSPEL-CENTERED

GLORY WOULD BEGIN TO **OVERWHELM** OUR COMMUNITIES.

LEADING THE
RADICAL STRATEGY

So far we've said every believer is essential to God's mission and every believer is equipped to engage in that mission by the power of the Holy Spirit. Another question we should ask at this point, if we want to be a church that's unleashed for radical mission, relates to church leadership.

Do you think there's a place for paid leaders in the church? Why or why not?

Read the following passages. Beside each one summarize the way church leaders should be treated.

1 Corinthians 9:8-18

Galatians 6:6

1 Timothy 5:17-18

When we look at the New Testament, we clearly see a warrant, even a command, to provide financially for certain teachers and leaders in the church. But what is their responsibility?

This is more than a question for pastors. It's a question for anyone in the body of Christ, because we're all responsible for the ministry of the church. In answering the question, though, we'll see that in many cases both leaders and followers have shifted a responsibility to leaders that shouldn't be theirs.

Read Ephesians 4:11-15. According to this passage, what is the job of church leaders?

Does this passage set a different expectation than most people have for church leaders? In what way?

What about you? What do you expect of your church leaders?

What do your church leaders expect of you?

According to this passage, God hasn't given leaders to the church to do the work of the Great Commission. We've already established that the Great Commission is for every believer. Rather, the responsibility of leaders is to equip God's people for ministry, preparing them to do works of service in Jesus' name.

God has entrusted the church with stewards of God's Word whose job is to equip God's people to be servants of God's Word. This understanding goes to the essence of being radical together, and it changes everything about the way we view leaders in the church.

Choose the option that best describes your expectations of leaders.

I expect my leaders to ▓ **provide services;** ▓ **equip people.**

What's the difference between those two options?

If you believe Ephesians 4, you need to make sure your expectations of church leaders fit. Leaders shouldn't be expected to spend their time organizing events that people can come to; they should spend their time organizing people for ministry. They should shove people out the door into the world instead of clamoring for them to come to one more activity.

Ephesians 4 shows us that the *preparation* for the work of ministry falls to church leaders. The *work* of ministry falls to everyone else.

How can you encourage your leaders in their work of equipping the church for ministry?

The difference between the two concepts of leadership is as simple as the difference between addition and multiplication. If a leader sees his job as doing the work of ministry, addition is taking place. And addition is a much slower way to increase influence and impact than multiplication.

If church members free their leaders to be equippers, big things start happening. Disciples begin to make disciples. And those disciples make disciples. With that vision it's not idealistic to dream that the church of God, unleashed for His purpose, might actually reach the ends of the earth with the gospel.

IT'S NOT IDEALISTIC AT ALL. JESUS SAID

THAT'S WHAT WOULD HAPPEN.

RADICAL
VISION

Welcome back to this small-group discussion of *Radical*.

What struck you as new or interesting from week 4 of the workbook? What questions do you have?

Describe what you like best about your church. In what ways have you been blessed by participating in church life?

David wrote, "You have the Word of God before you, the Spirit of God in you, and the command of God to you: make disciples of all nations." How do you react to that statement?

What talents and resources do you possess that can be used to advance God's kingdom?

To prepare to view the DVD segment, read aloud Isaiah 61:1-3:

> *"The Spirit of the Lord God is on Me,*
> *because the Lord has anointed Me*
> *to bring good news to the poor.*
> *He has sent Me to heal the brokenhearted,*
> *to proclaim liberty to the captives*
> *and freedom to the prisoners;*
> *to proclaim the year of the Lord's favor,*
> *and the day of our God's vengeance;*
> *to comfort all who mourn,*
> *to provide for those who mourn in Zion;*
> *to give them a crown of beauty instead of ashes,*
> *festive oil instead of mourning,*
> *and splendid clothes instead of despair.*
> *And they will be called righteous trees,*
> *planted by the Lord*
> *to glorify Him."*

WATCH

Complete the viewer guide below as you watch DVD session 5.

A Divine Contrast

God responds to the needs of the poor with _____.

God responds to those who neglect the poor with _____.

Those who indulge themselves and ignore the poor will stand _____ before God.

We are the _____ _____.

An Eternal Consequence

If we indulge ourselves and neglect the poor, earth will be our _____.

Eternity will be our _____.

A Clear Choice

Continue in hollow _____ that neglects the poor.

Caring for the poor is not an optional _____ in salvation.

Caring for the poor is necessary _____ of salvation.

You're absolutely justified by grace alone through faith alone, but it's a faith that radically transforms a _____. It transforms desires.

A Clear Choice

Turn in honest _____ to care for the poor.

Hear the Word _____.

Obey the Word _____.

We are not motivated to care for the poor by _____.

We are motivated to care for the poor by the _____.

We obey Christ not because we are guilty but because we are _____.

Video sessions available for purchase at *lifeway.com/radical*

Following David's DVD teaching segment is the story of a couple that is obeying God's command to care for the poor.

Discuss the DVD teaching segment with your group, using the questions below.

What question would you most like to have answered after watching the DVD segment?

David said, "Jesus is speaking to religious people who are so blinded by their affluence, the love of money, that they justified their affluence in the middle of their religious devotion." How do you react to that statement?

Describe a time in recent years when you did something to help those who are poor. What do you remember most about that experience?

Describe a time in recent years when you neglected or ignored the needs of the poor. What do you remember most about that experience?

How can we determine whether we are neglecting the poor in our current lifestyles?

David said, "You'll be able to tell by the way people are giving to the poor whether Christ is in them." How do you fare when measured by that standard? What's a big step you can take in the coming weeks to obey Christ's commands about the poor?

Suggested Scripture memory for this week:

> *"You know the grace of our Lord Jesus Christ: Though He was rich, for your sake He became poor, so that by His poverty you might become rich"* **(2 Cor. 8:9).**

Read week 5 and complete the activities before the next group experience. Consider going deeper into this content by reading chapters 7 and 8 in David Platt's book *Radical* and chapter 5 in *Radical Together.*

RADICAL
VISION

Every year in the United States we spend more than $10 billion on church buildings. In America alone the amount of real estate owned by institutional churches is worth more than $230 billion.

Numbers like that should lead us to question our priorities, especially since so much of the rest of the world lives in abject poverty. In fact, if you and I have running water, shelter over our heads, clothes to wear, food to eat, and transportation, then we're in the top 15 percent of the world's people in terms of wealth.

We're rich. The very fact that you're doing this study is a testament to your wealth. Our riches aren't just in terms of finances either. We're spiritually rich with our abundance of churches, preachers, podcasts, and Christian literature.

With all of these resources at our disposal, it's time for us to ask the very serious question of vision. Are we committed to further accumulation, or will we have the vision to do what Jesus has called us to do?

FROM BEGINNING TO END

If you ask any Christian what their mission is, hopefully they'd respond with something similar to what Jesus said in Matthew 28:19-20: "Go, therefore, and make disciples of all nations, baptizing them in the name of the Father and of the Son and of the Holy Spirit, teaching them to observe everything I have commanded you. And remember, I am with you always, to the end of the age."

What many of us fail to realize, however, is that this is the Great Commission; it's not the New Commission.

Do you think of the Great Commission as an exclusively New Testament idea? Why or why not?

Can you think of an Old Testament passage that might express a similar command?

The fact that we often don't connect the Great Commission to the Old Testament is to be expected; many of us, whether or not we acknowledge it, operate under the assumption that there are basically two Gods in the Bible.

There's the Old Testament God who commanded holy war and swallowed up the disobedient with fire and earthquakes. And then there's the God of the New Testament, a God of love, mercy, and grace. Such a dichotomy is more than just bad theology; it's theology with drastically bad side effects, whether we believe it explicitly or implicitly.

What side effects might there be in your spiritual life if you make a distinction between an Old Testament God and a New Testament God?

God is the same "yesterday, today, and forever" (Heb. 13:8). Theologians call this attribute of God His immutability; He doesn't change. When you think about it, it only makes sense. Why does anyone change? It's because that person wants to become better or different than he or she once was. If God altered His operations or character in the four hundred years between Malachi and Matthew, the implication is that in the previous years He was somehow imperfect.

Further, if God changed then, who's to say He might not change again? Do you see it? If we think of God in the New Testament as different from God in the Old Testament, we attack the perfection of the holy God. We then remove any sense of security we might have that comes in knowing God never makes mistakes or operates in anything less than absolute perfection.

But if it's true that the God of the Old Testament is the same God of the New Testament, it means when Jesus commissioned His first followers, He did so as an extension of what God had already been doing in the previous centuries. One of the clearest places we see God's work of redemption in the Old Testament is in Genesis 12, the call of Abram.

Read Genesis 12:1-3 and list ways God promised to bless Abram.

Look closely at verse 3. For what purpose was God blessing Abram?

How does God's purpose in these verses relate to Jesus' Great Commission?

Abram was the father of the Jewish nation. He was the beginning of God's special people, those He would set apart for Himself. But it's essential that we see in this passage that God didn't bless Abram or His descendants for their own sake. He wouldn't shower them with blessings so that they could be more comfortable. He blessed them for the sake of all nations on earth:

> *All the peoples of the earth*
> *will be blessed through you.*
> *Genesis 12:3*

When God blessed Abram, the rest of the world was on His mind. Way back in the Old Testament.

Read the way Paul reflected on this passage in Galatians 3:6-14. Who are the children of Abraham, according to this passage?

What is the blessing that the children of Abraham are meant to extend?

God promised Abraham land. He promised him protection. But more than anything else, the greatest blessing God gave to Abraham was the same blessing He gives to every child of Abraham today—Himself. That's the true blessing.

As children of Abraham, we've been blessed with the knowledge of God in Jesus Christ. Jesus is the ultimate fulfillment of this centuries-old promise of blessing for God's people, as well as the means by which God wants to bless all nations on earth. Jesus is at the center of Genesis 12.

The same charge is for us today. We haven't been given the blessing of new life in Christ so that we can appreciate being blessed. We've been blessed in order to be a blessing to others.

THAT'S THE CORE OF THE GREAT COMMISSION:

IT'S THE MISSION TO FULFILL THE DESIRE OF GOD

FROM THE BEGINNING TO **BLESS** THE NATIONS

OF THE EARTH WITH THE KNOWLEDGE OF HIMSELF.

"I'M NOT CALLED"

I wonder whether, in some ways intentionally and in other ways unknowingly, we've erected lines of defense against the global purpose God has for our lives. It's not uncommon to hear Christians say, "Not everyone is called to international missions" or more specifically, "I'm not called to international missions." In this mind-set missions is a compartmentalized program of the church, and select Christians are passionate about and effective in missions. The rest of us are willing to watch the missions slideshows when the missionaries come home, but God hasn't called most of us to go on mission.

Have you ever claimed not to be called to missions? When? Why?

What are some ways we justify our lack of involvement in God's global cause?

When we read and believe the Bible, it forces us to have a radical vision for the world. We can't relegate the global cause of Christ to a select few, hiding behind our checkbooks or a once-a-year mission trip. Instead, we must begin to ask ourselves, *How can I lead my life, my family, and my business to be on mission for God's glory around the world?*

If we start asking that question, we show that we're no longer content to sit on the sidelines while a supposed special class of Christians accomplishes the global cause of God. We show that we're convinced God has created us to make His glory known in all nations, and we're committing our lives to accomplish that purpose.

Read Romans 1:14-15. What do you think Paul meant by calling himself a debtor to the nations?

How does this assertion relate to the cause of global evangelism?

Paul literally said, "I'm in debt to Jews and Gentiles." The language is profound. Paul said he owed a debt to every lost person on the face of the planet. Because Christ owned him, Paul owed Christ to the world.

Every person this side of heaven owes the gospel to every lost person this side of hell. We owe Christ to the world—to the least person and the greatest person, to the richest person and the poorest person, to the best person and the worst person. We're in debt to the nations. In our contemporary approach to missions, though, we've subtly taken ourselves out from under the weight of a lost and dying world, wrung our hands in pious concern, and said, "I'm sorry. I'm just not called to that."

Read the progression of ideas Paul set forth in Romans 10:11-15 and fill in the blanks.

A person calls on whom they _____. They believe when they _____. They hear when someone _____. And someone preaches when they are _____.

This progression is the way the nations come to share in the blessings of the knowledge of God. Every believer in Jesus Christ is commanded to be involved in this process.

Working backward from verse 15, you see that God's plan involves sending His servants. So that's step 1 in God's plan: God sends servants. Then, continuing backward in the passage, you see that those servants preach the gospel. Every servant of God is intended to go and proclaim the gospel. This is God's plan. He sends servants, and His servants preach.

Moving one step further back, when His servants preach, people hear. When they hear, they believe. Now this passage isn't teaching that every person who hears the gospel will believe it. But it's teaching that when we preach and people hear, some will believe. And the Book of Revelation promises that one day every nation, tribe, and language will be represented before the throne of Christ (see 7:9). This means every people group will hear the gospel preached and someone from every people group will trust in Christ for salvation.

Does this truth give you confidence to go on mission? Why or why not?

The last two steps in God's plan are obvious. When hearers believe, they call on the name of Jesus. When they do that, they are saved. It's simple. But before we end today's lesson, think about one key question.

At what point is this process most likely to break down?

Think about it. It's not in the calling. It's not in the hearing. It's not in God's sending. There's only one potential breakdown point in this progression: when God's servants don't preach the gospel to all people.

WE ARE THE PLAN OF GOD. THERE'S NO PLAN B.

DAY 3

THE POOR OUTSIDE THE GATE

We are blessed to be a blessing. God has shown us the riches of His grace in Christ so that we can declare those riches to the very ends of the earth.

Anyone wanting to proclaim the glory of Christ to the ends of the earth must consider, though, not only how to declare the gospel verbally but also how to demonstrate the gospel visibly in a world where so many are urgently hungry. If we're going to address urgent spiritual needs by sharing the gospel of Christ or building up the body of Christ around the world, we can't overlook dire physical needs in the process.

Why do you think God cares so much about the poor?

Can you think of any biblical texts that talk specifically about the poor?

Read Matthew 25:42-46. How closely does God identify Himself with the poor?

Why, then, do you think most of us consistently neglect the poor?

Nowhere does the Bible teach that caring for the poor is a means by which we earn salvation; the basis of salvation is the work of Christ alone. But that doesn't mean our use of wealth is totally disconnected from our salvation.

Read James 2:14-26. According to this passage, how is our care for the poor connected to our salvation?

The faith in Christ that saves us from our sins involves an internal transformation that has external implications. According to Jesus, you can tell someone is a follower of Christ by the fruit of his or her life, and the writers of the New Testament show us that the fruit of faith involves compassion for the material needs of the poor.

A story recorded in Luke 16 reveals how serious God considers caring for the poor to be.

Read Luke 16:19-31. How does this story reveal God's care for the poor?

Don't miss the fact that Jesus told this story to a group of religious leaders who loved money and justified their indulgences. He told them about a rich man who lived in luxury while he ignored a poor man, Lazarus, who sat outside his gate, covered with sores and surrounded by dogs, eating the scraps that fell from the rich man's table.

When both men died, the rich man went to hell, while the poor man went to heaven.

Lazarus's name literally means *God is my help*. Sick, crippled, and impoverished, Lazarus received compassion from God. Of course, Lazarus didn't go to heaven because he was poor, and the rich man didn't go to hell because he had money. Both were there because of their faith or their lack thereof.

The rich man demonstrated his lack of faith by indulging in luxuries while ignoring the poor outside his gate. As a result, earth was his heaven, and eternity became his hell.

When you hear this story, with whom do you identify more—Lazarus or the rich man?

Honestly, how concerned are you with the poor outside your gate?

Whether or not you've recognized them yet, the poor are there. Today more than a billion people in the world live and die in desperate poverty. They attempt to survive on less than a dollar a day. Close to two billion others live on less than two dollars a day. That's nearly half the world struggling to survive on the same amount we spend on French fries.

More than 26,000 children today will breathe their last breath due to starvation or a preventable disease. Do you feel the weight of those statistics? God does. And He's calling the church to stop living in luxury to the neglect of the poor. If you believe in the gospel and you've been made new in Christ, you have to respond.

GOD **DEMANDS** IT.

THE DIFFICULTY OF RICHES

Despite the scriptural demands for Christians to demonstrate the gospel by caring for the poor, it's frightening to think many of us have turned a blind eye to the realities of the world.

We have a very willing ignorance not only about the poor but also about their powerlessness. Literally millions of them are dying in obscurity while we enjoy our affluence and pretend they don't exist.

Think about the times during a regular day when you come in contact with the poor or powerless. What are those contact points? News stories? Street corners? News sites? List them below.

Are you prone to ignore them? Why do you think that is?

Like Lazarus, the poor and powerless are outside our gates. And they are hungry. In the time we gather for worship on a Sunday morning, almost a thousand children elsewhere die because they have no food. We certainly wouldn't ignore our own kids while we sang songs and entertained ourselves, but we're content ignoring other parents' kids. Many of them are our spiritual brothers and sisters in developing nations. They're suffering from malnutrition, deformed bodies and brains, and preventable diseases. At most we're throwing our scraps to them while we indulge in our pleasures here.

This isn't what the people of God are supposed to do.

Read 1 John 3:16-18. What are the people of God responsible to do, according to this passage?

Although passages like these are clear, why do you think we seem to have a blind spot for the poor?

When we study the truth of God's Word and see the need around us in the world, the people of God will respond with the compassion of Christ. But from the beginning, the riches of God's people have been dangerous.

Read Mark 10:23-24. How did the disciples react when Jesus gave His command to the rich young ruler?

Why do you think they were so surprised?

In that culture God's blessing was equated with material possessions. That's one way God blessed Abraham, David, and Solomon. It was through material blessing that the people of God first built the beautiful temple in Jerusalem. But with the coming of Jesus, a new phase in redemptive history was unfolding. No teacher in the New Testament ever promised material wealth as a reward for obedience.

In the New Testament the people were the temple where God's Spirit dwelled; they were no longer meant to build a majestic place of worship. Instead, followers of Jesus were to devote their resources to building people, not a place.

Read 1 Timothy 6:6-9. Why did Paul say possessions can be dangerous?

What's the alternative lifestyle, according to these verses?

How does this teaching relate to Jesus' statements about wealth in Mark 10?

Most of us in our culture and in the American church simply don't believe Jesus or Paul on this one. We don't believe our wealth can be a barrier to entering the kingdom of God. We are fine with thinking of affluence, comfort, and material possessions as blessings but certainly not as barriers. We think the way the world thinks: that wealth is always to our advantage. But Jesus said the exact opposite: that wealth can be a dangerous obstacle.

How can wealth be an obstacle to our involvement in God's mission today?

In the context of Paul's passage above, contentment is described as having food and clothing, that is, having the necessities of life. Then verse 9 warns that those who desire to be rich and acquire more than life's necessities are in danger of being plunged into ruin and destruction.

Do you see once again how loving Jesus' command to the rich young man really was? He wasn't trying to rob Him; He was trying to protect Him from the dangers of wealth. But like children who refuse our parents' instructions to eat broccoli because we want to eat only candy, we cry foul against Jesus.

A radical vision for the world requires a correspondingly radical vision for our possessions. If we want that kind of vision, we need to ask whether we're willing to be content with food and clothing, having the basic necessities of life, or …

DO WE WANT **MORE?**

FINISH THE MISSION

How much is enough for the church?

This is an important question if we want to be radically committed to finishing the work Jesus left for us. I'm not assuming you and I can singlehandedly give enough to alleviate poverty, just as you and I can't singlehandedly tell every nation the gospel of Jesus Christ. We can affect some, even in small ways, even if others are beyond our influence. Clearly, God doesn't command or expect us to meet every need. But the logic that says, "I can't do everything, so I won't do anything" is straight from hell.

Read Luke 21:1-4. What principle of giving did Jesus emphasize?

How is that different from the way most of us give of ourselves?

The picture here is of sacrificial giving. That's a radical departure from the way we generally operate. But what if we began to give not just what we're able but beyond what we're able? What if we did that not only with our material possessions but also with our influence? Our time? Our commitment?

What if we saw the mission of Jesus in the world as being that important?

This is the call on the church, not just because of the critical physical and spiritual needs around us but because this kind of giving is actually what the heart of Christ in us demands and desires.

Read 1 Timothy 6:6-18. How does this passage relate to the widow in Luke 21?

How would giving like this free us from the deadly nature of wealth and possessions?

This kind of giving is real freedom. It's the kind of freedom that can be experienced only by those who are radically seeking to follow Jesus' commands. It's the kind of freedom that's rooted in faith, because it doesn't feel good at first for anyone to start selling their possessions for the sake of Christ. But you do it anyway, not because it feels good but because your actions are firmly rooted in the belief that Jesus actually knows what He's talking about.

What you find is that Jesus was never trying to rob you of joy and pleasure; He was pushing you into it.

Completing the mission of Christ will take this kind of sacrifice. In fact, completing that mission, at least for the American church, is a war. It's a constant battle to resist the temptation to have more luxuries, to acquire more stuff, and to live more comfortably. It requires strong, steady resolve to live out the gospel in the middle of an American Dream that identifies success as moving up the ladder, getting a bigger house, purchasing a nicer car, buying better clothes, eating finer food, and acquiring more things.

What are three practical ways you will engage in this war?

1.

2.

3.

Maybe you need to downsize your home. Maybe you need to begin the adoption process. Maybe you need to set a budget that frees you to give more to overseas missions. Maybe you need to pack up and move yourself. The point is that in wartime everyone makes sacrifices. It's necessary to ask these questions if we want to finish the task.

Read Matthew 24:14. What is Jesus' return contingent on?

What does our love for material possessions reveal about the seriousness with which we take this passage?

There's no time to waste. The church has already wasted enough time. We sit around asking what God's will is for our lives when Scripture has clearly laid it out for us. The question is not, Can we find God's will? The question is, Will we obey God's will?

Will we refuse to sit back and wait for some tingly feeling to go down our spines before we rise up and do what God has already commanded us to do? Will we risk everything—our comfort, our possessions, our safety, our security, our very lives—to make the gospel known among the nations?

WILL WE **REPRIORITIZE** EVERYTHING IN THE CHURCH TO THAT END INSTEAD OF MAKING OURSELVES MORE COMFORTABLE?

WEEK 6
RADICAL
GOD

Welcome back to this small-group discussion of *Radical*.

What struck you as new or interesting from week 5 of the workbook? What questions do you have?

David wrote, "Every person this side of heaven owes the gospel to every lost person this side of hell." How do you react to that statement? What does it mean for your practical, everyday life?

Is guilt a positive or negative emotion? Why?

Have your attitudes and actions toward the poor changed over the course of this study? If so, how?

To prepare to view the DVD segment, read aloud John 15:9-17:

> *"As the Father has loved Me, I have also loved you. Remain in My love. If you keep My commands you will remain in My love, just as I have kept My Father's commands and remain in His love. I have spoken these things to you so that My joy may be in you and your joy may be complete. This is My command: Love one another as I have loved you. No one has greater love than this, that someone would lay down his life for his friends. You are My friends if you do what I command you. I do not call you slaves anymore, because a slave doesn't know what his master is doing. I have called you friends, because I have made known to you everything I have heard from My Father. You did not choose Me, but I chose you. I appointed you that you should go out and produce fruit and that your fruit should remain, so that whatever you ask the Father in My name, He will give you. This is what I command you: Love one another."*

WATCH

Complete the viewer guide below as you watch DVD session 6.

We do not compare; Jesus' life is our _____.

We do not despair; Jesus' presence is our _____.

Christ has never called you to be _____ _____. He has said,
"I'm the only One who can make you good enough."

Ask God to bring these truths to _____ in you.

Avoid apathy; Jesus' words are our _____.

It's not an option to be _____ to the words of Christ if you're a follower
of Christ.

To be a follower of Christ means to come to an awareness of your sinful _____
against God, to see in Jesus the only substitute for your sins, by His grace to turn from your
rebellion against God, and to trust in Him as the Lord and sovereign _____ over your life.

What Jesus says determines how you _____.

Avoid lethargy; Jesus' glory is our _____.

We're in a fight, a race, a battle, and a _____.

We want the _____ and the _____ to experience His glory.

Video sessions available for purchase at *lifeway.com/radical*

Following David's DVD teaching segment is the story of a couple that is adopting a radical lifestyle and living for the glory of God.

Discuss the DVD teaching segment with your group, using the questions below.

What did you like most about the DVD segment? Why?

What have you appreciated most about this study as a whole? Why?

What questions or issues would you like the group to address before concluding this study?

Review the four principles David emphasized during the DVD segment:

• We do not compare; Jesus' life is our standard.

• We do not despair; Jesus' presence is our hope.

• Avoid apathy; Jesus' words are our authority.

• Avoid lethargy; Jesus' glory is our goal.

Which principle are you most thankful for? Why?

Which principle will be most difficult for you to follow? Why?

David said, "It is not possible to be a follower of Christ and be indifferent to what Jesus says, because whatever He says determines how you live." Take a moment to examine your life and determine whether you are currently being indifferent to any of Jesus' commands that you've explored in this study. If so, consider asking the group to pray for you right now.

Suggested Scripture memory for this week:

"I am the vine; you are the branches. The one who remains in Me and I in him produces much fruit, because you can do nothing without Me" (John 15:5).

Read week 6 and complete the activities to conclude this study. Consider going deeper into this content by reading chapters 3 and 4 in David Platt's book *Radical* and chapter 6 in *Radical Together*.

RADICAL
GOD

By this point, by God's grace, you're beginning to feel the pull toward something bigger and greater. You've seen Jesus' radical demands for you and your church, and you're realizing that most of us need to seriously reshape our priorities and reorder our lives.

This isn't because you've participated in this study. It's because you're being gripped by an overwhelming God. You're realizing you belong to a God who desires, deserves, and demands absolute devotion in your life and your church, and now you want to give Him nothing less. He's worthy of your all—your life, budget, ambition, church programs, relationships, possessions, career, and trust.

As Christians united with one another in the church, we are selfless followers of a self-centered God.

DAY 1
SELFLESS FOLLOWERS,
SELF-CENTERED GOD

We are selfless followers of a self-centered God.

Reflect on that statement. Does it bother you? Why or why not?

In what sense are we selfless?

In what sense is God self-centered?

The Christian life is about dying to self. It's about giving up the right to determine the direction of our lives. Our God is our Lord, our Master, and our King. He holds our lives in His hands, and He is free to spend them in whatever way He pleases.

Several years ago many churches debated whether someone could know Jesus as Savior without knowing Him as Lord. This, at the heart, is really a question of authority. Could someone trust in Christ for eternal salvation and yet not recognize His authority in their lives by their absolute obedience?

The question of authority was often asked of Jesus during His earthly ministry.

Read Luke 20:1-8. Why do you think these people were concerned about Jesus' authority?

Why do you think Jesus didn't answer their question?

Jesus walked, talked, taught, and healed with power and authority. He didn't need to appeal to anyone else to justify His teachings; He *was* the authority. But to the religious leaders in this passage, that authority was threatening. If Jesus' authority was from heaven, they knew they had an obligation to obey.

Authority is like that. If you recognize that someone has authority, then suddenly that person has a claim on your life. Jesus knew it too, and that's why He didn't answer the religious leaders' questions outright. Jesus knew they had ulterior motives in challenging His authority, but He isn't interested in theoretical questions and mind games. He's looking for followers.

Are there any areas of your life you haven't submitted to Jesus' authority?

To recognize the authority of Christ is to submit to the authority of Christ. To put it in terms of the argument about Jesus being Savior and Lord, there's no difference. There's no Jesus except the Lord Jesus. To follow Jesus at all is to follow Him completely. That's what it means to be selfless.

But to call God selfish? We might bristle at a suggestion like this. But over and over again, the Bible teaches us that God acts in His own self-interest.

Read Genesis 1:27-28. How does God's command to fill the earth relate to His pursuit of His glory?

God gave His people His image for a reason: so that they could multiply His image throughout the world. He created human beings not only to enjoy His grace in a relationship with Him but also to extend His glory to the ends of the earth.

Read the following passages. Write beside each reference the reason behind God's actions.

Exodus 14:4

Psalm 23:3

Isaiah 43:1-13

Daniel 3:28-29

Revelation 7:9-10

At the beginning of earthly history, God's purpose was to bless His people so that all people would glorify Him for His salvation. At the end of history, God's purpose will be fulfilled. Individuals from every nation, tribe, people, and language will bow down around His throne and sing praises to the One who has blessed them with salvation. This is the final, ultimate, all-consuming, glorious, guaranteed, overwhelming purpose of God in Scripture.

God is seeking His own glory from the entire world. It's the great *why* of God.

IF WE WANT TO FOLLOW THE RADICAL GOD, THEN,

WE MUST HAVE THE SAME CORE DESIRE IN OUR **HEARTS**.

DAY 2
JESUS DIDN'T DIE
ONLY FOR YOU

We live in a church culture that has a dangerous tendency to disconnect the grace of God from the glory of God. Our hearts resonate with the idea of enjoying God's grace. We bask in sermons, conferences, music, and books that exalt a grace centered on us. And though the wonder of grace is worthy of our attention, if that grace is disconnected from its purpose, the sad result is a self-centered Christianity that bypasses the heart of God.

Have you ever considered that grace might have a higher purpose than just you?

Think back to your study yesterday. What might that higher purpose be?

If you asked the average Christian sitting in a worship service on Sunday morning to summarize the message of Christianity, you would most likely hear something along the lines of "The message of Christianity is that God loves me."

As wonderful as this sentiment sounds, is it biblical?

How would you summarize the message of Christianity?

If "God loves me" is the message of Christianity, who's the object of Christianity? It's I.

Therefore, when I look for a church, I look for music that best fits *me* and programs that best cater to *me* and *my* family. When I make plans for *my* life and *my* career, it's about what works best for *me.* Though this version of Christianity largely prevails in our culture, it's not biblical.

The biblical message of Christianity is not "God loves me" but "God loves me so that I can make Him known among all nations." Scripture shows that God is the object of our faith, and Christianity centers on Him. We aren't the purpose behind the gospel; God is.

God focuses on Himself, even in our salvation. He saves us not for our sake but for the sake of His holy name (see Ezek. 36:22). God loves us for *His* sake in the world.

Is that shocking to you? Why or why not?

Does that mean God doesn't love us deeply?

The fact that God is zealous for His glory doesn't mean He isn't passionate about His people. It does mean, however, that His passion doesn't ultimately center on His people. It centers on His greatness, His goodness, and His glory being made known globally among all peoples. One of the clearest expressions of this truth is in Paul's description of salvation in Romans 3.

Read Romans 3:23-26. Are you familiar with this passage? Any one part more than others?

Look closely at the passage. Why did God offer Jesus as an atoning sacrifice for our sins?

Where do you see God's commitment to His glory in this passage?

These verses offer us an appropriately God-centered view of the cross. They also counter many of our trite sayings that accompany our reflections on Jesus' death. We can't necessarily say we were on Jesus' mind as He died that day, but we know for sure that God was.

Jesus died for God. Because God is perfectly just and sin is atrocious rebellion against His perfect character, in His justice He must dispense a proportionate punishment against sin. If He didn't, He would compromise His perfect character. So the choice for God was to punish justly all of humankind or to punish Jesus. In His wisdom and grace He chose the latter.

Jesus knew this. He accepted this. He willingly offered Himself to be crushed under the weight of sin. The result is that God is both gloriously just and, at the same time, the glorious justifier of those who put their faith in His Son.

The Bible makes clear that God's desire for His own glory is infused into His every action. And wondrously, we get to be a part of that. It sounds radical to our ears, but to follow Jesus is to commit ourselves to the mission of God.

THAT MISSION IS CENTERED ON HIMSELF.

A NEW VISION

The only possible vision for the church of Jesus Christ is to make known God's glory in all nations. This must drive our churches because this is what drives God. Far more than we want stuff for the church, crowds at the church, or activities in the church, we want to know, love, honor, and praise God. And we want all people to do the same. We want to see God glorified by people everywhere because God wants to see Himself glorified by people everywhere.

If you had to sum up the vision of your local church in one statement, what would it be?

How closely does that vision align with God's pursuit of His own glory?

What might have to change in your church if it began to align its purpose with God's purpose?

What happens when our vision in the church changes? What happens when our primary aim is not to make the crowds feel comfortable but to exalt God in all His glory? Suddenly our priorities begin to change. More than we want people to be impressed by the stuff we can manufacture, we want them to be amazed by the God they can't fathom. More than wanting to dazzle them with our production, we want to direct them to His praise. And the last thing we want to do is raise up people who are casual in the worship of God as they sit back and enjoy a cup of coffee.

Instead, we want to raise up people who are so awed, so captivated, so mesmerized by the glory of God that they will gladly put down their coffee—and lay down their lives—to make His greatness known in the world.

Think practically about your own church, particularly the following areas. Beside each, list one way such a vision might affect it.

Budget:

Worship:

Children's ministry:

Special events:

We should guard against a temptation here. If God is seizing your heart with His greatness and you're looking around at your fellowship, perhaps you're seeing some discrepancies. Maybe you see many of the same tendencies in your church that have characterized your life.

So do you leave? Find a new church? Go to a different church that's aligned more closely with this new vision? Although such a move might be necessary in some cases, in most cases you will want to stay in your church to be a catalyst for change.

Perhaps the focus of your imagination doesn't need to be on a different church but on what your church might be.

Read 1 Corinthians 14:22-25. According to this passage, how is an unbeliever brought to Christ in the church?

The vision for a church that's committed to following God is that it's completely, uncompromisingly enthralled with Him. When unbelievers enter the church, they're so captivated by His greatness displayed there that they cry out to know Him too.

Unleashing God's people to accomplish God's purpose in the world requires that we devote ourselves to relentless prayer in the church. Why? Because prayer is one of the primary demonstrations of our selflessness and God's self-centeredness. As it's often been said, prayer isn't preparation for the work. ...

PRAYER IS THE WORK.

DAY 4
A CONSTANT DEPENDENCE

We must pray for our churches. In our selflessness you and I realize it's impossible to see change in our churches, much less accomplish God's purpose, in our own strength. So we express our dependence on God in prayer, and He delights in showing His glory by giving us what we need to accomplish His purpose.

Why is prayer, by its very nature, an expression of dependence on God?

Read Psalm 50:15, a description of prayer at its core. According to this passage, what do we do in prayer?

What does God do and receive when we pray?

Through prayer God gives grace to His children in a way that also brings glory to Him. Prayer is a nonnegotiable priority for any church or church member who wants to follow God.

Read each of the following passages. What do they have in common?

Acts 1:14

Acts 2:42

Acts 6:4

What does this practice reveal about the priorities of the local church?

The early church was utterly dependent on God's power. Many of the church's breakthroughs in the Book of Acts came about as a direct result of prayer. God often performed mighty works for the propagation of the gospel and the declaration of His glory in response to the prayers of His people.

These believers knew prayer was necessary to accomplish God's purpose in the world. The point of prayer isn't to carry on business as usual in the church. The reality is, we can conduct monotonous, human-centered religion on our own. But if we want to make disciples in all nations, we need to pray. For when we sacrifice everything we are and stake everything we have on the front lines of a battle for the souls of millions of people around us and billions of people around the world who don't know Jesus, we are forced to pray.

Pray for your church. Pray that it will catch a vision for the greatness of God. Spiritual victories are beyond us, and we should realize their enormity and our inadequacy to achieve them. The greatness of our task makes us aware of our desperate need for God, and we should live in constant, desperate dependence on Him.

Read Isaiah 62:6-7. How does this passage relate to prayer?

Specifically, how does this passage relate to the urgency of prayer?

"Do not give Him rest" (v. 7). I want to be part of a people who are giving God no rest from our praying to and seeking Him. I want to be part of a people who are calling on the Lord day and night, refusing to leave Him alone because we hunger for God's Word in our lives, God's power in His church, and God's glory in all nations.

I want to give God no rest until our churches are fully committed to the great and glorious purpose of God. I want to give God no rest until we experience His power and presence as we see in the church in Acts. One man preached, and more than three thousand people were cut to the heart and saved. Every day the Lord added people to the church who were being saved. The lame were walking, and the blind were seeing. Thousands were coming to Christ at great cost, yet they couldn't be prevented from proclaiming the gospel. God was picking up people and planting them in remote deserts to talk to people who were wondering about Jesus. The number of disciples was growing rapidly, and the gospel was spreading with power.

I WANT TO BE PART OF A WORK OF GOD LIKE THAT. DO YOU?

WORTH THE RISK

Matthew 10 is a sobering reminder that a radical life is a risky undertaking. But in this warning let's remember that for many in the world, this isn't a picture of something radical.

It's normal.

Read Matthew 10:16-25. What's the most sobering part of this passage to you?

What do you find encouraging in this passage?

The language in these verses envisions Jesus as a military commander sending soldiers out on a mission. He summoned His disciples and sent them out. In light of the needs before them and the danger around them, the disciples knew they were entering battle.

Do you have that same sense of urgency about Jesus' commands?

What in your life might be dulling that sense of urgency?

In the late 1940s the United States government commissioned the building of an $80 million troop carrier for the navy. The purpose was to design a ship that could speedily carry 15,000 troops during times of war. By 1952 construction on the SS *United States* was complete. The ship could travel at 44 knots and could steam 10,000 miles without stopping for fuel or supplies. It was the fastest and most reliable troop carrier in the world.

The only catch is, it never carried troops.

Instead, the SS *United States* became a luxury liner for presidents, heads of state, and a variety of other celebrities who traveled on it during its 17 years of service. As a luxury liner, it couldn't carry 15,000 people. Instead, it could house just under 2,000 passengers. Those passengers could enjoy the luxuries of 695 staterooms, 4 dining salons, 3 bars, 2 theaters, 5 acres of open deck with a heated pool, 19 elevators, and other comforts of the world's first fully air-conditioned passenger ship. Instead of a vessel used for battle during wartime, the SS *United States* became a means of indulgence for wealthy patrons who desired to coast peacefully across the Atlantic.

How did the goals of the troop carrier contrast with the goals of the luxury liner?

How do you think this example might relate to the church today?

Read Matthew 16:16-19. How do Jesus' wartime instructions in Matthew 10 line up with His description of the church?

The church was designed for battle. The church's purpose is to mobilize a people to accomplish a mission. Yet we seem to have turned the church from a troop carrier to a luxury liner. We seem to have organized ourselves not to engage in battle for the souls of peoples around the world but to indulge ourselves in the peaceful comforts of the world.

Reread the previous sentence. Is that true of your church? Why or why not?

We need more than a renewed commitment to the radical but biblical commands of Jesus. We need God to open our eyes to the war waging around us. Things change in wartime. Priorities are different. Values are shifted. And we're in a war for the glory of God.

May God give us the courage and conviction to look squarely in the face of a world with 4.5 billion people going to hell and 26,000 children dying every day of starvation and preventable disease. If we saw the need and we were gripped by the greatness of God, we would decide it's time to move this ship into battle instead of sitting back on the pool deck and waiting for the staff to serve us more hors d'oeuvres.

Let's get serious. Let's get real. Let's embrace the great God and His great mission. Imagine not just an individual but the entire church of Jesus Christ, which we know will overcome in the end, committed and mobilized for the sake of His glory among all nations. Imagine it.

NOW **THAT** WOULD BE **RADICAL**.

WHAT IS JESUS WORTH TO YOU?

If anyone would come after me, he must deny himself and take up his cross and follow me.
MATTHEW 16:24

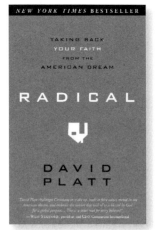

In *Radical,* David Platt challenges Christians to consider with an open heart how we have manipulated the gospel to fit our cultural preferences. He shows what Jesus actually said about being his disciple—then invites you to believe and obey what you have heard.

RADICAL COMMUNITIES OF FAITH

Platt examines how the right understanding of the church in six critical areas fuels radical obedience among Christians and offers guidance to help church members, leaders, and pastors apply the revolutionary claims and commands of Christ in fresh practical ways to their communities of faith.

Includes small group discussion guide.

MINISTRY TOOLS

*Introductory booklets, based on **Radical** and **Radical Together.***

Available in packs of 10, ideal for small group distribution or church welcome packages.

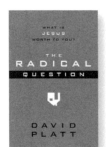

The Radical Question

David Platt reveals what can happen when we exchange our convenient beliefs for authentic discipleship.

A Radical Idea

Go further. Platt explores the radical idea that when ordinary believers mobilize in everyday ministry, communities will be changed dramatically.

WATERBROOK MULTNOMAH
PUBLISHING GROUP